THE
CHRISTIAN
LIFE

WITNESS LEE

Living Stream Ministry
Anaheim, CA • www.lsm.org

First Edition, December 1994.

ISBN 978-0-87083-820-0

Published by

Living Stream Ministry
2431 W. La Palma Ave., Anaheim, CA 92801 U.S.A.
P. O. Box 2121, Anaheim, CA 92814 U.S.A.

Printed in the United States of America

06   07   08   09   10   11   /   11   10   9   8   7   6   5

CONTENTS

PREFACE

This book is composed of messages given by Brother Witness Lee in Anaheim, California from February 21 to June 19, 1992.

CHAPTER ONE

THE DEFINITION

Scripture Reading: Phil. 1:20b-21a; John 14:10-20, 6a; 3:36;
Heb. 7:16b; 2 Tim. 1:10b; Col. 3:4a; John 11:25; Rom. 8:2a, 9b;
Gal. 2:20; Rom. 12:5; Eph. 1:23; 3:19; Matt. 5:13-16; Eph.
3:8-11

In this series of messages, we want to fellowship concerning the Christian life. Such a topic may seem common to us, but I must honestly tell you that to my impression it is very hard to find one believer that knows what the Christian life is. The Bible is a very complicated book. Some fundamentalists say that the Bible does not contradict itself. But the more we study the Bible, the more contradictions we find in it. We have to realize that in the whole universe if there is no contradiction, nothing can remain, nothing can exist. All things exist by contradiction. Do we always laugh? We laugh and we also weep. Someone may say, "I am a happy person." But this is not completely true because this person is also full of anxiety.

To know the Christian life is not an easy thing. Do you believe that the apostle Paul was always victorious? Today among us we have a saying—"Revived every morning; overcoming every day." Do you believe you can be revived every morning and overcoming every day? If within a day you do not have any defeat to match your victory, you actually do not have a good day. Can anyone among us say that we had one day in our entire life which was full of victory with no defeat? Today we are in the "kitchen" of the Christian life. While a meal is being cooked in a kitchen, everything is a mess there. Today our experience is in the kitchen, not on the dining table. In our Christian life, when everything is cooked and put on the dining table, that will be the New Jerusalem. In our present experience, however, the New Jerusalem seems mostly like a "bird in the air." I have spoken much about the New Jerusalem, but this New Jerusalem "bird" has never been fully in my hand even though it is always in my expectation.

The Christian life is a mystery. I cannot tell you that I know what the Christian life is in an absolute way. Some may ask, "Since you don't know, why do you speak about it?" I am still endeavoring to know. On the one hand, I say that I do not know. On the other hand, I can say that I do know what the Christian life is to some extent. We need to see what the Christian life is from the Bible. Furthermore, I hope that what I have seen and experienced in the Christian life can be a help to you.

In this message, I want to cover two main points. The first point is that the Christian life is the life in which the believers of Christ live Christ and magnify Christ. The second point is that the Christian life is the life in which the Christians live Christ and magnify Him corporately in their locality as a local church to be a local expression of Christ as a part of the universal Body of Christ. The Christian life is and should always be in these two aspects—the individual aspect and the corporate aspect. We need to live an individual Christian life for a corporate Christian life. The corporate Christian life is the church life. This refers specifically to the local church. If we do not have a local church life, we cannot experience anything of the universal Body of Christ.

Now I would like to point out why I said that the Bible is contradicting. This is because the truths of the Bible are not written and presented in an orderly sequence. Instead these truths are here and there, scattered, throughout the Bible (cf. Isa. 28:13). The Bible is like a great jigsaw puzzle with many small parts, but all of these parts are scattered. The Bible does not arrange the truths in a certain sequence, putting the parts together to present a full and perfect picture. We have to gather the many parts of a truth to see it in a complete way. In your study you may have picked up ten parts, but none of these parts are connected to one another. Every part stands by itself. You need to spend time to collect more parts of the puzzle and put them together gradually.

I have been studying the Bible for over sixty-five years. I have found that it is very difficult to put the parts of the Bible together. We should not just hold one part and think that this is everything. We have to be patient and go on to pick up more and more parts until we have a complete view. In the past thirty years, there were times when I thought that I had put all the parts of the Bible together. I thought I had a completed jigsaw puzzle. But eventually there was still something more. Through the help of others' understanding of the Bible, I have put many parts of the Bible together, but I cannot tell you that I have finished. I have spoken much throughout the years concerning the Divine Trinity. This is because the parts in the Bible concerning the Divine Trinity are scattered from the first chapter of Genesis to the last chapter of the book of Revelation. In this series of messages, we want to put together the parts of the Word concerning the Christian life so that we can see what the Christian life is.

I. THE CHRISTIAN LIFE BEING THE LIFE IN WHICH THE BELIEVERS OF CHRIST LIVE CHRIST AND MAGNIFY HIM

The Christian life is the life in which the believers of Christ live Christ and magnify Him. This is based upon Philippians 1:20-21a, which says, "According to my earnest expectation and hope that in nothing I will be put to shame, but with all boldness, as always, even now Christ will be magnified in my body, whether through life or through death. For to me, to live is Christ." Paul said that for him to live was Christ. This means that we need to live Christ. If we add a preposition to the phrase to live Christ, this changes the meaning. To live out Christ, to live by Christ, to live through Christ, to live with Christ, and to live in Christ are not quite the same in meaning as to live Christ. According to my knowledge, I never heard anyone use this term—to live Christ. This describes the fact that Paul's life was to live Christ. He lived Christ because Christ lived in him (Gal. 2:20).

The term to live Christ bears a particular significance. We

are here to live Christ. We are not just living by Him, living with Him, living in Him, or living Him out. We are living Christ, and this living of Christ is for us to magnify Him, to make Him larger in others' eyes. Paul was confined in prison. He was fearful that he might not magnify Christ, not make Christ larger; he could have made Christ small in the eyes of those observing him. Paul desired, even in prison, to make Christ bigger, to make Christ larger, to magnify Christ.

The Christian life is not merely an ethical life, a good life, or a moral life. The Christian life, of course, should be ethical, moral, and excellent. But strictly speaking, it is not an ethical life. It is something higher than an ethical life. The Christian life is a life that lives Christ. In our living as a Christian, others should not see merely our goodness, our ethics, or our morality. They should see Christ. We Christians should live a life that lives Christ and magnifies Him.

A. Christ Being
the Center of the Divine Trinity

Christ is the center of the Godhead. The Godhead is the Divine Trinity—the Father, the Son, and the Spirit—and Christ is the center of the Divine Trinity. As the center of the Divine Trinity, Christ expresses the Father and is realized as the Spirit (John 14:10-20).

What is it for Christ to express the Father and be realized as the Spirit? In the four Gospels, we see a wonderful person by the name of Jesus. He spoke the Father's word (John 14:10, 24) and did the Father's work (John 4:34; 17:4). He did whatever the Father did (John 5:19). John 14 shows that the Son is the embodiment and expression of the Father (vv. 7-11) and that the Spirit is the reality and realization of the Son (vv. 17-20). Christ is the Son, and He is the Father (Isa. 9:6; John 14:8-9). He is also the Spirit (2 Cor. 3:17; 1 Cor. 15:45b). When He was in His earthly ministry, many knew that He was a Nazarene and the son of Mary. Yet He was also the embodiment of the Triune God. He was the Son who was with the Father (John 8:29; 16:32) and by the Spirit (Luke 1:35; Matt. 1:18, 20; 12:28). He did everything with the Father and by the Spirit. He expressed God the Father, acted by the Spirit, and was eventually realized as the Spirit. In the Gospels, we can see the Father, Son, and Spirit in one person, Jesus. This is the One whom we need to live as our mysterious life.

B. This Christ Being the Life

This Christ is the life, the unique life, and no other life is the real life (John 14:6a). The Christ who is the Father, the Son, and the Spirit is the life. *Contradiction if we look @ it seperately. But*

At the end of Matthew, the Lord charged the disciples to *they're the* go and baptize people into the name of the Father and of *same not* the Son and of the Holy Spirit (28:19). But in the Acts and the *contradictory* Epistles we cannot find this saying again. Acts says that they baptized people into the name of the Lord Jesus (8:16; 19:5), and Romans 6:3 and Galatians 3:27 speak of being baptized into Christ. This shows that Jesus Christ is the Father, the Son, and the Spirit. To baptize people into the name of the Lord Jesus and into Christ equals and is to baptize people into the name of the Father, the Son, and the Spirit. Therefore, Jesus Christ is the Father, the Son, and the Spirit.

A person's full name is actually composed of three names—the first name, the middle name, and the last name. This is following the pattern of the Triune God. One God has three titles—God the Father, God the Son, and God the Spirit. As the embodiment of the Triune God, Christ is the life, the unique life. No other life is the real life (1 Tim. 6:19b).

C. Christ Being the Eternal Life

Christ is the eternal life, eternal in time, quality, perfection, and completion, indestructible and incorruptible (John 3:36; Heb. 7:16b; 2 Tim. 1:10b). Everyone who believes into the Son, Christ, has eternal life. The life which Christ is, is eternal. Christ is perfect, not temporarily but eternally. Christ is also eternally and entirely complete. With us human beings, nothing is eternal or entirely complete.

Many immigrants who come to the United States try to get permanent residence here, but who is permanent? Very few have lived in the United States for over a hundred years. Everyone eventually departs because human life is temporary. To God one thousand years equals one day (2 Pet. *We're not eternal (100 yrs on earth is only 1/100 of 1 day in Gods eyes). We're only perfect in parts, not entirely complete. not perfect as a whole.*

3:8). Thus, one hundred years is only one-tenth of a day in God's sight. To remain somewhere for only one-tenth of a day is not permanent. God, however, lives from eternity to eternity. Psalm 90 speaks of this. This psalm actually was the first psalm written because it was written by Moses. In Psalm 90:1 Moses said, "Lord, You have been our dwelling place in all generations." Then he said, "From eternity to eternity You are God" (v. 2). This means that Moses realized that God was his eternal dwelling place. From eternity to eternity, He is God and He is our dwelling place. He is eternally perfect and complete. Even though we are not able to reside on this earth permanently, we already have a permanent residence in God, the eternal One.

The eternal life, Christ, is also eternal in quality. In quality this life is eternally good. The quality of our human life, using Jeremiah's word, is like broken cisterns (Jer. 2:13). Our qualities are all broken qualities. We may be clever, but our cleverness has been broken into pieces. Our human life, unlike the divine life, is not eternal in quality.

The eternal life is also indestructible and incorruptible. We human beings can be destroyed by anything, and we are corruptible in ourselves. I have some old books written by Brother Nee. As time goes on, they are corrupting. Today I dare not touch some of these books, for fear that they will fall apart. Time wasted these books because they are corruptible. We also become old and pass away because we are corruptible. Our nature is corruptible. But Christ, the One who is our life, is incorruptible.

D. Christ Being Life to His Believers in Resurrection

Christ is life to His believers in resurrection (Col. 3:4a; John 11:25). Resurrection means that this life has gone through death. People put this life into death, and this life came out of death. Today He is a life in resurrection.

E. Christ Being in the Believers as the Spirit of Life

Christ is in the believers as the Spirit of life (Rom. 8:2a, 9b).

THE DEFINITION

He is the Spirit (2 Cor. 3:17; 1 Cor. 15:45b). When I came to this country about thirty years ago, I began to tell people that Christ is the Spirit. There are a number of hymns we wrote in our hymnal concerning experiencing Christ as the Spirit (see *Hymns*, #493, #539). Brother Nee wrote some of these hymns, which stress that <u>the very Christ, whom we experience today as the life that we live, is the Spirit</u> (#490, #491, #492).

F. Christ Living in the Believers
That They May Live by Him

Christ lives in the believers that they may live by Him (Gal. 2:20). We need to be clear that it is not wrong to say that we live by Christ. But we need to see that <u>to live by Christ</u> different signifies one thing and <u>to live Christ</u> signifies another thing. <u>Christ lives in us so that we may live by Him.</u>

G. The Believers Who Live Him,
as Such a One,
Being His Living Members,
Constituting His Organic Body

The believers who live Him as such a One are His living members, constituting His organic Body. First, we constitute His Body as the fullness of Christ, the One who fills all in all, as His expression (Rom. 12:5; Eph. 1:23). Then we constitute His Body as the fullness of the Triune God, the God who has been processed and consummated, as His corporate expression in the expression of Christ through the church (Eph. 3:19). These are two layers of expression. We as a corporate church are the expression of Christ. Then in the expression of Christ there is another layer of expression, that is, the expression of the processed and consummated Triune God.

When the church came into existence, that indicated that God had completed His process and that He had been consummated. <u>Before God's incarnation, He had never been processed.</u> God has gone through a long process from incarnation to ascension. Within a short time of less than thirty-five years, He completed this long process. We all need to speak about the wonderful process through which the Triune God passed.

By His being processed from incarnation to His ascension, He was consummated. His work to produce the new creation began from His incarnation, and that work was consummated in His ascension. He came down from heaven to be incarnated, and He went back to heaven in ascension. But after going back, He was altogether a "different" God. Some may wonder how we could say this, but there is such a fact. Before His incarnation, He did not possess the human nature. But after passing through the process of incarnation through ascension, He now has both divinity and humanity. Before His incarnation, He did not possess such a wonderful death and surpassing resurrection. But today after His ascension, this death and resurrection are now elements in His composition.

The church does not express the God who has not been processed, but the church expresses the very God who has completed His process and has been consummated. The church can express Him because the church has become the same as He is. He is divine and human, and the church is human and divine. He possesses a marvelous death and an excellent resurrection, and the church possesses the same. The church is the same as He is, but the church does not have His Godhead. The church has the nature of God, the life of God, and the very death and resurrection which God possesses. The church is the same as God in all these things, but not in the Godhead. The church as the organic Body of Christ is the fullness of the Triune God, the God who has been processed and consummated. We are Christ's living members, constituting His organic Body to express Him.

II. THE CHRISTIAN LIFE BEING ALSO THE LIFE IN WHICH THE CHRISTIANS LIVE CHRIST AND MAGNIFY HIM CORPORATELY

The Christian life is also the life in which the Christians live Christ and magnify Him corporately in their locality as a local church to be a local expression of Christ as a part of the universal Body of Christ. The Christian life must be a church life. The Christian life should not be just an individual Christian life. It should be a corporate Christian life, the church life. Wherever you are on this earth, you should participate in the local church there.

Many of us in the Lord's recovery are very church-conscious. But actually very few Christians today are church-conscious. They do not have any consciousness concerning the church. If there were no local church on this earth, I would not know how to live, how to exist. We all are a part of a local church, and every local church is a part of the universal church, which is the Body of Christ.

The Christian life is not just to live an ethical life with the human virtues, as the salt of the earth and the light of the world, for the glory of God (Matt. 5:13-16), but to live a life that is Christ Himself with His divine attributes expressed in His human virtues to be a part of His organic Body for the universal consummation of the eternal economy of God (Eph. 3:8-11). Christianity teaches that we must have human virtues. Because we are a Christian, we are the salt of the earth and the light of the world. The world is rotten and corrupt, so there is the need of salt to kill the germs. The world is also dark and needs the light to enlighten it. This is all for the glory of God. This is a good teaching, but we must realize that the individual Christian life occupies just a small part of the Christian life. The greater part of the Christian life should be the church life.

In the church life, we live a life that is Christ Himself with His divine attributes expressed in His human virtues. His attributes are divine, but His virtues are human. The human virtues are to manifest the divine attributes, and the divine attributes are to be expressed in the human virtues. This is for us to be a part of His organic Body. We live a life that is Christ Himself not just for the individual Christian life, but for the Body life. We live as parts of His organic Body for the universal consummation of the eternal economy of God.

Recently, I spoke about the human and divine concepts in Psalms 1 and 2 (see *Life-Study of the Psalms*—Message One). We have seen that Psalm 1 is not concerning God's economy. It concerns only the personal benefit of the individual godly man. But Psalm 2 is altogether concerning God's economy. This psalm says God made Christ His Anointed (v. 2). God set up Christ as His King (v. 6) to inherit all the nations and to possess the earth to gain a great kingdom on this earth for God's economy (vv. 8-11). We have to believe in such a Christ, taking Him as our refuge. We also have to love Him, to kiss Him (v. 12). This concerns God's economy. All that most Christians think about is their personal benefit. To them salvation is only a matter of either going to heaven or perishing in the lake of fire. There is no consideration about God's economy. But Psalm 2 reveals that Christ is altogether for God's economy. We have to believe in Him, to take refuge in Him, and we have to love Him, to kiss Him.

We also have to admit that much of our consideration is for our personal benefit. We may consider whether we will receive a reward from Christ when He returns or be punished by Him. We do not consider God's economy that much. The entire book of Psalms, from the first point to the last point, reveals that Christ is altogether for God's economy. He died for us to accomplish God's economy. He saves us to accomplish God's economy. He also lives in us that we may live in Him for God's economy. This is why we are not only the church, the Body of Christ, but also the kingdom of Christ, of God. The kingdom of God is the accomplishment of God's economy. We all have to realize that the Christian life is a life that is for God's economy.

CHAPTER TWO

THE CONTENTS

Scripture Reading: John 14:6-20; Matt. 28:19; 2 Cor. 13:14; Acts 16:7; Phil. 1:19b; Heb. 9:26, 28; Rom. 6:6; Gal. 5:24; Heb. 2:14; John 12:31; Eph. 2:15; Col. 1:20; John 12:24; Acts 13:33; 1 Pet. 1:3; 1 Cor. 15:45b; Eph. 1:20-21; Exo. 30:22-31; John 7:39; 2 Cor. 3:17; Gal. 3:14; Rev. 2:7; 22:17

In the first message, we fellowshipped concerning the definition of the Christian life. We saw that the Christian life is the life in which the believers of Christ live Christ and magnify Him (Phil. 1:20b-21a). It is also the life in which the Christians live Christ and magnify Him corporately in their locality as a local church to be a local expression of Christ as a part of the universal Body of Christ. The Christ whom the believers are living and magnifying is the center of the Divine Trinity. Why do we say that Christ is the center of the Divine Trinity? He is the center, on the one hand, to express the Father, and on the other hand, to be realized as the Spirit (John 14:6-20).

These two phrases—*to express the Father* and *to be realized as the Spirit*—are short, but they are crucial. To arrive at the second phrase, *to be realized as the Spirit,* took me probably more than fifty years. It was not until these past fifteen years of my ministry that I began to use this phrase. The phrase *to express the Father* was used not only by us but also by others. Many fundamental theologians would agree that Christ the Son is the expression of the Father. But to say that Christ the Son is realized as the Spirit brings us into a big war. Some have said that this is heresy, but this is the truth revealed in the holy Word. This truth is very mysterious. To say that the

Second of the Divine Trinity is realized as the Third is the ultimate understanding of the Divine Trinity.

In this message we want to see the contents of the Christian life. The contents of the Christian life is not a simple matter. To know the contents of the Christian life, we have to know the sixty-six books of the entire Bible. Now I would like to ask, "What is the content of the Christian life?" The content of the Christian life is the entire Bible. I want to help us realize this in a very simple way. The first verse of the Bible says, "In the beginning God created the heavens and the earth" (Gen. 1:1—ASV). The last verse of the Bible says, "The grace of the Lord Jesus be with all the saints. Amen" (Rev. 22:21). The Bible is one book. It begins with God, and it ends with the Lord Jesus. Are God and the Lord Jesus two or one? If you say they are two, this is not logical. How can a book start with God and end with another person?

The Bible as the content of the Christian life is the autobiography of the Triune God. The Triune God has written a record of His own history, which we should call the autobiography of the Triune God. Who is God? What is God? What has God done, what is He doing, and what will He do? Where was God, where is God, and where will God be? There is only one autobiography which speaks of God, and this autobiography is the content of the Christian life. Thus, the content of the Christian life is altogether not simple.

When I was very young, I read the Old Testament, including the minor prophets. But I did not spend much time to study these minor prophets. In the upcoming summer training of 1992, we will have a life-study of these minor prophets. There are twelve minor prophets, but we will cover eleven of them since we have already covered Zechariah. Recently, I was working on the outlines for Hosea. Hosea is a very difficult book to read. Most of his writing is in poetic form. Verses 4 through 7 of Hosea 7 speak of the symbols of an oven and a baker. These symbols are particularly difficult to understand and interpret. I am sharing this so that we can realize that the Bible is altogether not that simple. It is too high, too deep, and too profound. The Bible is an autobiography, not a history. It is not a compiled book of theological doctrines and teachings.

The Bible is an autobiography of a wonderful person—the processed and consummated Triune God. This wonderful person comprises many things.

I. THE PROCESSED AND CONSUMMATED TRIUNE GOD

The processed and consummated Triune God is revealed in John 14:6-20. These fifteen verses are the very center of this divine autobiography. They bring us to the center of this person whose autobiography is the Bible. We say that Christ is the center of the Divine Trinity, expressing the Father and being realized as the Spirit, based upon these fifteen verses. I learned from others that the Son expresses the Father. But I did not learn from others that the Son is realized as the Spirit. I discovered this in the divine revelation of the Scriptures.

Our Christian life is a person. His autobiography is our biography. The Bible is the Triune God's autobiography, and before we experience it, it is our biography. But after experiencing it, it becomes our autobiography. In our Christian life, we Christians are all writing our autobiography. We are writing our autobiography by copying what is written in God's autobiography. Eventually, the apostle Paul's autobiography was just the Bible.

The Triune God as a wonderful person is the contents of our Christian life. He exists from eternity to eternity, having no beginning or ending. As such an eternal One, He created the universe and man. After His creation of man, He remained the same for four thousand years. One day in time, He entered into a long "tunnel" to get Himself processed. That long tunnel, or long process, lasted a little more than thirty-three and a half years.

After passing through such a process, He became different. Before those thirty-three and a half years, He was only divine, not human. But after those thirty-three and a half years, He became both divine and human. In other words, before that process He was only God, not man. But after that process, He became both God and man. Thus, some particular element was added into Him, and that particular element was humanity.

Before His incarnation, He had divinity, but He did not have humanity. It was in incarnation that He picked up humanity and put humanity upon Himself. In His resurrection He brought this humanity with Him, and He uplifted this humanity to make this humanity a divine humanity. Now in His ascension, He is both divine and human, having both divinity and humanity. These are the basic elements of His person, and these basic personal elements are the basic contents of the Christian life.

In His process He passed through incarnation, and He also passed through a living that lasted over thirty-three years. No one can fathom the mysterious human living of this God-man. He was the very Triune God, *Elohim* (Hebrew—Gen. 1:1), who created the universe, coming to pick up humanity and living in this humanity on earth for thirty-three and a half years. Who can imagine this? Most Christians have never spent time to muse on God's human living. We have to consider such a great thing. God became a man and lived in His humanity on this earth continually for thirty-three and a half years. He never left during this period of time. Today we take vacations, but He never had a vacation in His human living. His human living is a great element of what He is today.

Many people move around in the course of their lifetime, but the Lord Jesus lived thirty-three and a half years altogether in the small area of Palestine. This is very meaningful. To live in a place under a certain kind of environment makes you a particular person. After living on this earth for thirty-three and a half years, God became very particular. He lived with a lot of odd people. These odd people were around Him all the time. He talked to these odd people and dealt with them. Peter and the other disciples were odd. Are we not odd also? I believe that all these odd people helped to "remodel" Him. We cannot deny that after living on earth for thirty-three and a half years, He spontaneously added another element to Himself, the element of human living. For God to live on earth among the odd people for thirty-three and a half years is a great thing.

Colossians 3:10 And have put on the new man, which is being renewed unto full knowledge according to the image of Him who created him. Colossians 3:11 where there cannot be Greek and Jew, circumcision and uncircumcision, barbarian, Scythian, slave, free man, but Christ is all and in all.

After passing through human living, He entered into death. Death was a short part of the long tunnel of His process, but He accomplished much in this short part. He solved our problem of sin (Heb. 9:26) and sins (v. 28). He terminated our old man (Rom. 6:6), our flesh (Gal. 5:24), the entire old creation (Col. 1:20), Satan (Heb. 2:14), the world (John 12:31), and the ordinances (Eph. 2:15). There are many ordinances in the human race. The Japanese, the Chinese, and the Americans all have their particular ordinances, or customs. These ordinances are forms or ways of living and worship. These customs also include the accent of the language. Even today many dear brothers who are from Texas cannot avoid speaking in a Texan southern accent. The first time I heard "y'all" was when I made my first visit to Texas. Moreover, in the United States, people in the South refer to those in the North as Yankees. This is an example of the ordinances among people. Of course, today by the Lord's grace and also by the Lord's sovereignty, we all are here in the United States. The United States is famous as a "melting pot." But many people have been here for years, and the United States has not been successful in "melting" them.

Thank the Lord that among us in the recovery the feeling of discrimination does not exist that much. But I dare not to say that this is entirely gone from among us. It is a shame for there to be any distinction of culture or race among us. Paul told us in Colossians 3:10-11 that there is no room for any natural person in the new man, but Christ is all and in all. There are no Japanese, Americans, Greeks, Jews, Chinese, etc., in the new man. Paul's word in Colossians 3 means that there is no room for any natural person to exist in the new man. But we may still keep some rooms in our thinking for Yankees, for Texans, for Japanese, or for Chinese.

Even today among us we may categorize the brothers. In our mind there are many rooms for natural persons. We may think one brother is a Texan, another brother is a Yankee, another brother is from the Midwest, and another brother is from the Northwest. Other brothers to us are Californians, and in California there are the northern Californians, from the Bay Area, and the southern Californians. This attitude and feeling to categorize the brothers is wrong. According to Ephesians 2:15, Christ has abolished all the ordinances through His death.

In His all-inclusive death, He also accomplished a positive work. This work was His releasing of the divine life within Him as the grain of wheat (John 12:24). The divine life was concealed in His human shell. The cross broke His human shell, and the divine life within Him was released. His death was a life-releasing death. The death of Adam is dark, but the death of Christ is bright. According to the divine autobiography, His all-inclusive death has also become an element of His being. After this death, He entered into His marvelous resurrection with His ascension.

Today He is an all-inclusive person as the processed and consummated Triune God. He has divinity, humanity, human living, an all-inclusive death, and an all-inclusive resurrection. We have to add these five things together—divinity, humanity, human living, the all-inclusive death, and the all-inclusive resurrection. When these five things are added together, we have today's processed and consummated Triune God. This One is our God, our Redeemer, our Savior, our Lord, our Master, our Head, our reality, our life, our living, and our everything. If some ask us who our God is, we should tell them all of this.

My God is a composition. He is composed of divinity, humanity, human living, an all-inclusive death, and an all-inclusive resurrection to be my God, my Redeemer, my Savior, my Lord, my Master, my Head, my reality, my life, my living, and my everything. This is my God! Then I would ask, "Where is your God?" This God of such a wonderful composition is right now within us. He is also mingling Himself with us to make us exactly the same as He is in life, nature, element, and essence, but not in the Godhead. We have to see all of this; then we will have an all-inclusive view concerning the contents of the Christian life.

I would encourage us to dwell on this short fellowship. Many Christian books are not in the central line of God's New Testament economy. They are not helping to write "Christian biographies" according to the autobiography of the Triune God. Even we ourselves are not so clear concerning what the real Christian life is. This is why I am burdened to have such a line on the Christian life. The content of the Christian life is the processed and consummated Triune God. To be consummated is to be completed. It is to be wrought with something until there is a completion, an accomplishment of having been wrought.

A. Comprising the Divinity of God and the Humanity of the God-man

The Triune God as the content of our Christian life comprises the divinity of God in His Divine Trinity—the Father, the Son, and the Spirit (Matt. 28:19; 2 Cor. 13:14). He also comprises the humanity of the God-man Jesus in His incarnation (Acts 16:7; Phil. 1:19b).

B. Compounded with:

1. Christ's All-resolving and All-terminating Death

The processed and consummated Triune God is compounded with Christ's all-resolving and all-terminating death (Heb. 9:26, 28; Rom. 6:6; Gal. 5:24; Heb. 2:14; John 12:31; Eph. 2:15; Col. 1:20; John 12:24). It would be helpful to remember these Scripture references. Hebrews 9:26 refers to the resolving of sin. Christ was offered once to take care of sin. Then Hebrews 9:28 says that Christ's death took care of our sins. Romans 6:6 says that our old man has been crucified with Christ. Then Galatians 5:24 tells us that Christ's death crucified our flesh and its lusts. Hebrews 2:14 says that Christ's death has destroyed Satan, and John 12:31 says that His death judged the world. Ephesians 2:15 is the verse telling us that Christ's death has abolished all the ordinances. These ordinances include not only those set up by us human beings but also those ordained by God. All of the ordinances were taken away by Christ on the cross. Colossians 1:20 further reveals that Christ's death has taken care of all the created things. Through His death, all the lost created things were brought back to God and reconciled to God. The above verses show that Christ's death dealt with all of the negative things in the universe. John 12:24 is a verse on the positive side of Christ's death, telling us that Christ as the unique grain of wheat fell into the earth to die and bring forth many grains. This is the life-producing death.

2. Christ's All-producing Resurrection

The processed and consummated Triune God is also compounded with Christ's all-producing resurrection (Acts 13:33; 1 Pet. 1:3; 1 Cor. 15:45b). What was produced in Christ's resurrection? First, Christ was produced as the firstborn Son of God. Second, His resurrection produced the many sons of God to be the members which constitute the Body of Christ, the church. Finally, the life-giving Spirit was produced in His resurrection. Acts 13:33 shows that Christ as the only begotten Son of God was reborn in resurrection to be the firstborn Son of God. Then 1 Peter 1:3 unveils to us that we, the believers of Christ, were born in Christ's resurrection to be the many sons of God. Finally, 1 Corinthians 15:45b reveals that Christ as the last Adam became a life-giving Spirit in His resurrection. Thus, the resurrection of Christ produced these three main things—the firstborn Son of God, the many sons of God to be the members of Christ constituting His Body as the church, and the life-giving Spirit. This is why I say that this resurrection is the all-producing resurrection.

3. Christ's All-transcending Ascension

The processed and consummated Triune God is also compounded with Christ's all-transcending ascension (Eph. 1:20-21). There are many things which are negative to us as Christians. All the fallen angels in the air are negative to us. But Christ's ascension conquered and subdued all of these negative things. In His ascension, He transcended from the earth through the air to the third heaven far above all. Thus, we can see that the elements of the processed and consummated Triune God include His all-resolving and all-terminating death, His all-producing resurrection, and His all-transcending ascension. Christ as the center of the Triune God was compounded with His death, resurrection, and ascension.

4. Typified by the Compounded Holy Ointment in Exodus 30:22-31

This compounded person is typified by the compounded holy ointment in Exodus 30:22-31. The compounded ointment was not merely oil. It was an ointment. Olive oil as the basic unit was compounded with four spices—myrrh, cinnamon, calamus, and cassia. Messages one hundred fifty-seven through one hundred sixty-six in the *Life-study of Exodus* cover the truth concerning the compounded ointment. I would encourage you to read or study those messages. All the elements plus all the numbers related to the compounded ointment signify Christ's divinity, humanity, human life, death, and resurrection. Some Bible teachers recognized that the compounded ointment was a type of the Holy Spirit. But no Bible teacher in the past gave us an analysis of the compounded ointment in all of its aspects. Through our own study we saw that olive oil typifies the unique God, myrrh typifies the precious death of Christ, cinnamon typifies the sweetness and effectiveness of Christ's death, calamus typifies the precious resurrection of Christ, and cassia typifies the repelling power of Christ's resurrection. Our God today is the compounded God.

I began to speak on this beginning in 1954. In a training in Hong Kong in that year, I told people that today in the Spirit there is the death of Christ and the resurrection of Christ. I received some help from chapter five of Andrew Murray's masterpiece entitled *The Spirit of Christ,* in which he stressed that the Spirit today includes both divinity and humanity. Since I came to the United States, this vision of the Spirit as typified by the compounded ointment has become clearer and clearer. I believe that this revelation today is in the highlight, at "noontime."

II. ALL THE CONTENTS HAVING BEEN CONSUMMATED TO BE THE ALL-INCLUSIVE SPIRIT OF LIFE THROUGH CHRIST'S DEATH AND RESURRECTION

All the contents, the elements, of the processed and consummated Triune God have been compounded together and consummated to be the all-inclusive Spirit. This all-inclusive

Spirit is the consummated Triune God, the consummation of the Triune God, through Christ's death and resurrection (John 7:39; 1 Cor. 15:45b; 2 Cor. 3:17; Gal. 3:14; Rev. 2:7; 22:17). John 7:39 says that the Spirit was not yet, because Jesus had not yet been glorified. At that time in the Gospels, the Holy Spirit was there, the Spirit of God was there, but not *the* Spirit. This is because Christ had not yet been glorified. This means that Christ had not gone through His death and entered into His resurrection. Jesus was glorified when He was resurrected (Luke 24:26). First Corinthians 15:45b reveals that Christ as the last Adam became a life-giving Spirit in His resurrection. Second Corinthians 3:17 says that the Lord is the Spirit, and Galatians 3:14 says that this all-inclusive Spirit, the Spirit, is the blessing of the New Testament gospel. The blessing of the gospel is not merely redemption, the forgiveness of sins, justification, regeneration, or salvation. The blessing of the gospel is a person, and that person is the all-inclusive Spirit as the consummation of the processed and consummated Triune God.

III. THE ALL-INCLUSIVE SPIRIT AND CHRIST'S ALL-INCLUSIVE DEATH AND HIS ALL-INCLUSIVE RESURRECTION BECOMING THE THREE MAIN ELEMENTS OF THE LIFE BY WHICH THE BELIEVERS OF CHRIST LIVE THE CHRISTIAN LIFE FOR THE CHURCH LIFE

The all-inclusive Spirit and Christ's all-inclusive death and His all-inclusive resurrection have become the three main elements of the life by which the believers of Christ live the Christian life for the church life. Therefore, to know the Christian life, we have to know these three elements.

CHAPTER THREE

THE ALL-INCLUSIVE SPIRIT

Scripture Reading: John 4:24; Luke 1:35; Matt. 1:20b; 28:19; Gen. 1:2b; Matt. 12:28; Rom. 8:9a; 1 Cor. 15:45b; 2 Cor. 3:17, 18; Rom. 8:9b; Acts 16:7b; Phil. 1:19b; John 14:17; 15:26; 16:13; 1 John 5:6; Rom. 8:2; Acts 1:8; Luke 24:49; Exo. 30:22-31; Rev. 1:4c; 4:5b; 5:6; Zech. 3:9; 4:10; John 3:6b; 7:39; Rev. 22:17a

In the previous message, we saw the contents of the Christian life. The contents of the Christian life are the Triune God who has been processed and consummated to be the all-inclusive Spirit of life through Christ's death and resurrection. The Christian life actually is the composition of three all-inclusive things—the all-inclusive Spirit of Christ, the all-inclusive death of Christ, and the all-inclusive resurrection of Christ.

The all-inclusive Spirit of Christ is compounded with Christ's death and resurrection. This is typified by the holy ointment in Exodus 30:22-31. The holy ointment is a compound. It is olive oil compounded with four spices. The first spice, myrrh, signifies the death of Christ. The second spice, cinnamon, signifies the sweetness and effectiveness of Christ's death. Calamus, the third spice, signifies the precious resurrection of Christ. Cassia, the fourth spice, signifies the power of Christ's resurrection. Thus, in this type of the holy ointment there is one basic element compounded with another four elements. We cannot say that the four spices are compounded with the olive oil because the four spices are not basic elements. The basic element is the oil. Today with the compound Spirit, the basic element is the Spirit of God, which is signified by the olive oil. The one Spirit is compounded with the elements of Christ's death and resurrection.

We all have to learn these things, not merely as a biblical teaching but by our own experience. The most pitiful thing today among Christians is their poverty in life. A number of Christians may use the term *life* without really knowing what life is. *Christ is life* has become a slogan to them, but very few Christians really know what the Christian life is. We may say, "The Christian life is just Christ." This is absolutely right, but who is Christ? Perhaps we would say that Christ is Jesus, and Jesus is the Son of God in incarnation. This is right, but how could this Christ who is in the heavens be our life? Some may say that He can be our life through the Holy Spirit, but if you ask them who the Holy Spirit is, they will be forced to say that they do not know. I am sharing this to show us that very few know what the Christian life is. I trust that this series of messages will make us clear concerning what the Christian life is and bring us into the real experience of the Christian life.

I. GOD BEING SPIRIT

In this message we want to see fifteen crucial aspects concerning the all-inclusive Spirit. The first point concerning the Spirit is mentioned in John 4:24, which says that God is Spirit. The source of the all-inclusive Spirit is God, who is Spirit. The word *Spirit* in John 4:24 does not refer to God's person but to God's nature. This is like saying that a person's ring is gold. This means that gold is the nature of the ring. John 4:24 says, "God is Spirit." There is no article used in the Greek text in this verse. This is similar to saying, "Your ring is gold." No article, such as *the* or *a*, is needed before the word *gold* because it speaks about the nature. This is why John 4:24 simply says that God is Spirit. This means that God's divine substance is Spirit.

II. THE THIRD OF THE DIVINE TRINITY
BEING THE HOLY SPIRIT

The three in the Divine Trinity are the Father, the Son, and the Spirit. The Third of the Divine Trinity is the Holy Spirit (Luke 1:35; Matt. 1:20b; 28:19). I would like us to consider the importance of the Holy Spirit among the three in the Godhead. The sixty-six books of the Bible contain many important items. Is the most important item in Genesis or in Revelation? Genesis 2 speaks of a garden with a wonderful tree, the tree of life, and man was put in this garden. But at the end of the Bible, there is a wonderful city. Which is more important—the garden or the city? Surely the city is more important because the New Jerusalem is the ultimate consummation of the divine revelation in the holy Scriptures. Thus, according to the basic principle, the last is the most important. Among the three of the Trinity, the Spirit is the most important in the sense of His being the realization, application, and reaching of the Triune God to us.

We saw in the previous message that the Son is the center of the Divine Trinity, expressing the Father and being realized as the Spirit. This shows us that the Son is the axis. The Son is the link. Without the Son, we cannot see the Father; and without the Son, we cannot get the Spirit. If we have the Son, we have both the Father and the Spirit. This is the very important thought in John 14.

The Lord told His disciples that in His Father's house, there were many abodes and that He was going to prepare a place for them (v. 2). Then Thomas said, "Lord, we do not know where You are going; how can we know the way?" (v. 5). Then the Lord answered, "I am the way and the reality and the life; no one comes to the Father except through Me" (v. 6). The way to the Father is the Lord Jesus. Later, Philip said, "Lord, show us the Father and it is sufficient for us" (v. 8). Then the Lord said, "Have I been so long a time with you, and you have not known Me, Philip? He who has seen Me has seen the Father" (v. 9). This means that the Lord is the Father. The Son and the Father are one person. The Lord also said, "Believe Me that I am in the Father and the Father is in Me" (v. 11). Who can be in another person and the other person be in him? For someone to say that he is with another one and the other one is with him is easy to understand. John 1:1 says that in the beginning was the Word and the Word was with God. But then it goes on to say that the Word was God. First, the Word was "with" God; then eventually the Word "was" God. How can this be? This is the mystery in the book of John.

It seems that the Lord spoke in John 14 without caring whether the disciples understood Him or not. I do not believe that any of the twelve understood what He was talking about. The Lord said that when He spoke, the Father who abode in Him did His works (v. 10). The Lord went on to say, "I will ask the Father, and He will give you another Comforter, that He may be with you forever" (v. 16). Eventually, He said, "The Spirit of reality...abides with you and shall be in you....In that day you will know that I am in My Father, and you in Me, and I in you" (vv. 17, 20). This shows that the Spirit's being in the disciples is the Son's being in them.

This brief fellowship gives us an overview of the first twenty verses of John 14. What is the secret of the mystery of these twenty verses? The secret is that the three of the Triune God are one. The Bible scholars in the early church pointed out that God is triune, three-one. In mathematics there is not such a figure. Who understands what three-one is? Some teachers added the preposition in, saying that God is three in one. Something that is three in one must be some kind of compound. Three elements are compounded together to be one entity. To illustrate this we may consider water with tea and lemon added to it. These three elements are compounded together to be lemon tea. They are three in one. This may be a good illustration, but no illustration is adequate to explain the mystery of the Divine Trinity. The Divine Trinity is beyond the realm of human understanding. We simply have to take the scriptural revelation of the Triune God and experience it.

Not long after I was saved, I began to meet with a group of Brethren believers who taught strongly that we should pray to the Father in the name of the Son. They gave verses as a basis for their teaching, and I accepted it. I tried to practice what they taught. Formerly when I prayed, I simply said "Lord Jesus" or "Father" without thinking about whom I was addressing. After being taught that I should pray to the Father in the name of the Son, I corrected myself when I did not do this. Eventually, I was so bothered that it became difficult for me to pray. They stressed strongly that the Lord Jesus told us to ask the Father in His name. But in my experience, whenever I prayed, the Father was there, the Son was there, and the Spirit was there.

In my writing, I may need three helpers to assist me. Sometimes I need number one. Then after five minutes, I need number two. A little later I need number three. I have to make three phone calls to get these three helpers, but with the three in the Godhead, we do not need to make three calls. When one is here, all three are here. Our God is the three-one God. The all-inclusive Spirit is the Third of the Divine Trinity, and the Third today is the consummation of the three. If you have the Third, you have the Second and the First.

III. THE SPIRIT OF GOD

To see the all-inclusive Spirit, we need to begin with the Spirit of God (Gen. 1:2b; Matt. 12:28; Rom. 8:9a). The Spirit of God is first mentioned in Genesis 1:2. The phrase *the Spirit of God* is composed of two nouns plus the preposition *of*. In this phrase, *God* is in apposition to *Spirit*. Thus, the Spirit *of* God means that God is the Spirit, and the Spirit is God.

IV. THE SECOND OF THE DIVINE TRINITY IN THE FLESH, WHICH HE HAD PUT ON IN HIS INCARNATION, BECOMING A LIFE-GIVING SPIRIT

The Second of the Divine Trinity in the flesh which He had put on in His incarnation became a life-giving Spirit (1 Cor. 15:45b). The all-inclusive Spirit is also the life-giving Spirit, who is the transfiguration of Jesus Christ. The Third of the Divine Trinity today is the transfiguration of the Second who was in the flesh. In eternity past, the Father, the Son, and the Spirit had merely one element, the divine element. Later, the Second of the three put on the flesh, and the flesh is human. Thus, with the Triune God today there are two elements: the divine element and the human element.

In eternity Christ was merely divine. One day in time He came into the flesh. That means He put humanity upon Himself. Then He died and resurrected. Through His death and resurrection, He did not drop His humanity. Some theologians wrongly taught that Christ put off His human nature in His resurrection. The Scriptures tell us that in the evening on the day of His resurrection, He came to the disciples (John 20:19-20). He told them to touch Him and to see that He was not a ghost, a phantom. After His resurrection, they could see the wounds in His hands, His feet, and His side (Luke 24:36-40). The Lord told Thomas to see His hands and touch His wounded side (John 20:25, 27). This shows us that the Lord's body was not left in the tomb. His body came out of the tomb in His resurrection.

First Corinthians 15 tells us that in resurrection He brought His body into glory (vv. 42-44). Today we still have a body of humiliation. But the day will come when our body of humiliation will be transfigured into a body of glory (Phil. 3:21). We cannot fully understand this, but we can see an example of this in nature. A carnation seed grows up and eventually is transfigured into a beautiful blossom. The seed is transfigured into another shape.

When Christ was incarnated, He brought divinity into humanity. Then when He resurrected, He brought humanity into divinity. This is the divine traffic to bring God into man and to bring man into God. God and man, divinity and humanity, have been mingled together to be one. Now not only the Son is in humanity but also the Father and the Spirit are in humanity. All three of the Godhead are in humanity.

Before Christ's incarnation and resurrection, divinity and humanity were separate entities. But humanity and divinity were mingled together in Christ. Jesus is the mingling of divinity with humanity. In His incarnation divinity entered into humanity. In His resurrection humanity entered into divinity, and divinity was mingled and compounded with humanity. With the lemon tea, the water, the tea, and the lemon are no longer separate elements. When we drink this, we are drinking "lemon-tea-water." The water has been compounded with another two elements. Our God has also been compounded with humanity and with all the elements of the process through which He passed.

After His resurrection, the Lord Jesus charged His disciples to baptize people into the name of the Father, of the Son, and of the Holy Spirit. The Acts and the Epistles say that the disciples baptized people into the name of the Lord Jesus (Acts 8:16; 19:5) and into Christ (Rom. 6:3; Gal. 3:27). This is because Christ is the totality of the three of the Godhead. This is like saying that tea is the totality of water, lemon, and tea. In our baptizing of people, we may be too dogmatic. We may insist on saying, "Brother, we are baptizing you into the name of the Father, of the Son, and of the Spirit." To repeat this, however, can be dogmatic. It is better to say, "Brother, I'm baptizing you into Christ." Christ is the embodiment and totality of the Triune God.

The Triune God—the Father, the Son, and the Spirit—is mingled and compounded with humanity. The Son entered into humanity, and He brought this humanity into divinity. *Into divinity* means *into the Divine Trinity*. Today all three of the Godhead are involved with humanity. First Corinthians 15:45b says that the last Adam became a life-giving Spirit. The last Adam was Christ as a person in the flesh. This person in the flesh became a life-giving Spirit. The word *became* indicates mingling. Christ became a life-giving Spirit by the way of compounding, by the way of mingling. Thus, the life-giving Spirit is the mingling of divinity and humanity. With the lemon-tea-water, the spirit (the essence) of the tea and the spirit (the essence) of the lemon are in the water. The essence of lemon and the essence of tea cannot be seen, but they can be tasted. Today we cannot see how man is in God and God is in man, but these divine and human essences are mingled together and are included in the all-inclusive Spirit.

V. THE LORD (JESUS CHRIST) BEING THE SPIRIT

The Lord (Jesus Christ) is the Spirit. Second Corinthians 3:17 says, "The Lord is the Spirit." The Lord in this verse, according to the context of this section, must refer to Christ the Lord (2:12, 14-15, 17; 3:3-4, 14, 16; 4:5). Jesus Christ today is the Spirit. The Spirit is Christ, and Christ is the embodiment of the Triune God.

VI. THE LORD SPIRIT

The Lord Spirit (2 Cor. 3:18) is a compound title like *the Father God* and *the Lord Christ*. This means that the Spirit is the Lord.

VII. THE SPIRIT OF CHRIST

The Spirit of Christ, mentioned in Romans 8:9b, is related mainly to the Lord's resurrection.

VIII. THE SPIRIT OF JESUS

Acts 16:7b speaks of the Spirit of Jesus. This is the only verse that uses this specific term for the Spirit. *The Spirit of Jesus* is a particular expression concerning the Spirit of God and is related mainly to the Lord's humanity, and human living.

IX. THE SPIRIT OF JESUS CHRIST

The Spirit of Jesus Christ (Phil. 1:19b) refers to Christ both in His humanity and human living and in His resurrection.

X. THE SPIRIT OF REALITY

Such a Spirit is the Spirit of reality (John 14:17; 15:26; 16:13; 1 John 5:6). In the whole universe, only One is real—the Triune God. Only the Triune God is the reality. Today the Spirit is the reality because the Spirit is the real essence of the Triune God. More than forty years ago, I read a book by Brother Watchman Nee which said that the Spirit is the reality of the resurrection. Resurrection needs some reality and that reality is the Spirit. If you are not in the Spirit, you are not in resurrection.

The Spirit is also the reality of Christ's all-inclusive death. We must be crossed out. Our flesh, our natural humanity, should be put to death, and death ushers in resurrection. Without death, there is no resurrection. This is why the Christian life must be a life of the Spirit through the cross and into the resurrection of Christ.

XI. THE SPIRIT OF LIFE

The Spirit is the Spirit of life (Rom. 8:2). The Spirit of life is the reality of life, for this Spirit contains the element of the divine life. Actually, the Spirit Himself is life. If we have the Spirit, we have life.

XII. THE SPIRIT OF POWER

The Spirit is also the Spirit of power (Acts 1:8; Luke 24:49). The Spirit is not only life within essentially but also power without economically. If we want to receive the Pentecostal power, we need to go through the cross of Christ so that we can be brought into resurrection. Then we will experience the Spirit as our life inwardly and our power outwardly.

XIII. THE COMPOUND SPIRIT, TYPIFIED BY THE COMPOUND HOLY OINTMENT

The all-inclusive Spirit is the compound Spirit, typified by the compound holy ointment (Exo. 30:22-31). The compound ointment has olive oil as a base compounded with four spices, myrrh, cinnamon, calamus, and cassia. The numbers related to this compound ointment are very significant. The one unit of olive oil is compounded with four spices. One signifies the unique God, and four signifies the creatures. This shows that the unique God is compounded with man, the creature.

Furthermore, there are five substances in the ointment. Five in the Bible signifies responsibility. The Ten Commandments in Exodus 20 are divided into two groups of five, and the ten virgins in Matthew 25 are divided into two groups of five. Our hand has four fingers plus one thumb. The four fingers signify man and the one thumb signifies God. We, the four, plus God, the one, bear responsibility, five. Every day our hands bear responsibility. Without a thumb, how could we pick up our Bible? We need the four fingers plus the thumb to bear responsibility. In the same way, we need ourselves plus God to bear responsibility. Every day we need to have a "plus." Our "plus" is God.

Also the four spices of the compound ointment are divided into three units of five hundred shekels each. Five hundred means one unit of full responsibility, and three signifies the

Triune God. The three units of five hundred shekels each, in four spices, signify the Triune God in resurrection mingled with humanity to bear the full responsibility. The New Jerusalem is a city of the number twelve, which is three times four. The city has twelve gates, three gates on four sides (Rev. 21:12-13). The numbers three and four are seen in the compound ointment. The entire New Jerusalem is one city composed of the unique Triune God, signified by the olive oil, mingled with man, signified by the four spices. The Triune God today has been consummated to be such an all-inclusive Spirit with all the marvelous elements of His person and work.

When I was a young Christian, I read some books which pointed out from the Word that we have died with Christ (Rom. 6:8a). I asked myself how I could experience this. Then I was taught that I should reckon myself to be dead (Rom. 6:11). There is a hymn by A. B. Simpson which speaks of reckoning ourselves to be dead to sin (*Hymns*, #692). I tried to reckon myself to have died with Christ, but this did not work. Brother Watchman Nee taught that we should reckon ourselves as having died with Christ in his book entitled *The Normal Christian Life*. Eventually, however, Brother Nee discovered that we cannot experience Christ's death in Romans 6 unless we experience the Spirit in Romans 8. The death of Christ is in the Spirit. Let us use the illustration of the lemon tea again. Where is the lemon? It is in the water. Where is the tea? It is in the water. In like manner, where is Christ's death? It is in the Spirit. Where is Christ's resurrection? It is in the Spirit. Where is the Triune God? He is in the Spirit. In this message I am sharing how to experience the Christian life. Without this Spirit, we cannot experience the death of Christ and the resurrection of Christ. This Spirit is the compound of God, man, Christ's death, and Christ's resurrection.

XIV. THE SEVEN SPIRITS,
WHO ARE THE SEVEN EYES OF GOD
AND THE SEVEN EYES OF CHRIST

The seven Spirits are the seven eyes of God and the seven eyes of Christ (Rev. 1:4c; 4:5b; 5:6; Zech. 3:9; 4:10). The seven

Spirits are the sevenfold intensified Spirit. In essence and existence, God's Spirit is one; in the intensified function and work of God's operation, God's Spirit is sevenfold. In my home I have a seven-way lamp, which the brothers made for me. Each time the switch to this lamp is turned, the shining becomes brighter and brighter, more intensified. Many lamps today are three-way lamps, but today the all-inclusive Spirit is seven ways, that is, sevenfold intensified. This is for the Spirit to go forth into all the earth.

A number of brothers and sisters among us have recently gone to Russia. These dear brothers and sisters went in the intensified Spirit. I also believe that the ones who are now preparing to go to Russia are intensified in their spirit. We may be able to rest and take it easy here, but the ones who are going to Russia cannot take it easy. They have to go to encounter all kinds of troubles. Our brothers and sisters first went to Russia in October, at the beginning of winter. The Russians who have been brought into the church life were very grateful to the saints for coming to them in the deep winter. They said that no foreigners would come to their country to carry out a project in the winter because it is too cold. But the brothers and sisters came in the deep winter to help them. Often, a number of the brothers did not have the time to eat dinner because they were so busy. I believe that their spirit is intensified. Many of us here, on the other hand, are not intensified. We may come to the meetings in a loose, relaxed, and unexercised way. Among us, whose spirit is intensified? We are like the "four fingers" thinking that they can function without the "thumb," that is, without the Spirit.

Going out to foreign countries to carry out the gospel for God's economy is through the Spirit sent to all the world as the sevenfold intensified One. This Spirit is the seven lamps of fire before the throne, and the throne is for God's administration. No doubt, the sevenfold intensified Spirit is to carry out God's administration.

These seven Spirits are the seven eyes of God. Some have said that the three persons of the Godhead are separate. But according to the scriptural revelation, the Spirit is the eyes of God. In other words, the Third of the Trinity is the eyes of the

First. The eyes are for expressing the sentiment. When I look
at you, my eyes express my feeling, my sentiment, about you.
In addition, the eyes are for observing and transfusing. When
one person looks at another person, he transfuses his feeling
into that person. Thus, the eyes are for expressing, for observing, and for transfusing.

2 The seven Spirits are not only the eyes of God but also
the eyes of Christ. Thus, the Third of the Divine Trinity is the
eyes of the First and the Second. Zechariah 3:9 tells us Christ
is the engraved stone. Christ as the stone was engraved on
the cross for us, and on this stone there are seven eyes. The
seven Spirits are the seven eyes of Christ.

At the time when we are preaching the gospel, speaking
about Christ, the Spirit looks at us to transfuse us, to express
Christ's feeling about us, and to infuse His love into us. In
other words, on the crucified Christ, there are eyes expressing His sentiment concerning us. The eyes on the crucified
Christ infuse His feeling, His love, into us. By this infusion,
we become inspired. We feel that our Christ is so lovely and so
good. Our Savior, the crucified One, has seven eyes to express
His sentiment concerning us and to infuse His love into us.
The stone in Zechariah is not a bare stone, but a stone upon
which are seven living eyes. We are preaching a living stone
with living eyes to infuse Himself into us and to express His
dear sentiment into our feeling.

XV. THE SPIRIT

John 3:6b says that we have been born of the Spirit. John
7:39 says that before Christ was resurrected, the Spirit was
not yet. *The* Spirit is the processed Spirit, the consummated
Spirit. Before Christ's resurrection, the consummation of the
Spirit was not completed, so this Spirit was not yet. The Spirit
of God was in Genesis 1, but in John 7:39 *the* Spirit was not
yet because Jesus was not yet glorified. Jesus was glorified in
His resurrection (Luke 24:26). In resurrection Jesus in the
flesh became a life-giving Spirit, and that life-giving Spirit is
the Spirit. In Christ's resurrection the Spirit of the Triune God
was consummated in the Spirit (1 Cor. 15:45b). Eventually, He
will be the Spirit as the processed and consummated Triune

God to be one with the bride as the corporate, regenerated, and transformed tripartite man (Rev. 22:17a). The consummated Triune God and the transformed tripartite man will be married to be one heavenly, universal couple.

CHAPTER FOUR

THE FUNCTIONS
OF THE ALL-INCLUSIVE SPIRIT

(1)

Scripture Reading: John 16:7-11; 1 Pet. 1:2a; 1 Cor. 15:45b; 2 Cor. 3:6b; John 3:5-6; Rom. 6:19, 22; 15:16; Titus 3:5; 2 Cor. 3:18; Eph. 1:13, 14; 2 Cor. 1:22b; Rom. 8:11, 14; Gal. 5:18; John 15:26; 1 John 5:6; Rom. 8:16; Acts 9:31; Rom. 14:17; Acts 13:52.

The verses in the Scripture reading concerning the functions of the all-inclusive Spirit were selected from the entire New Testament. I would encourage us all, especially the young people, to remember all these verses. If possible, it would be good to learn to recite them. In each of these verses, there is a crucial word or phrase with which we must be impressed.

In the previous message, we saw fifteen items concerning the all-inclusive Spirit. The first item is that God is Spirit, and the last item is that the Spirit is the processed and consummated Triune God. These two items are the alpha and the omega of the points concerning the all-inclusive Spirit. The alpha is God being Spirit, and the omega is *the* Spirit. In this message we want to see the functions of the all-inclusive Spirit.

The functions of the all-inclusive Spirit involve God's economy in His Trinity. God is uniquely one, yet in His Godhead there are three. The Divine Trinity—the Father, the Son, and the Spirit—is for God's economy. Regretfully, the term *economy* is mostly missed today among Christians, even though it is strongly revealed in the New Testament, especially in Paul's writings (Eph. 1:10; 3:9; 1 Tim. 1:4). The Trinity is for God's

the more you speak, the more victorius you become.
function of the Spirit to carry out God's Economy.

economy, and God's economy is for His heart's desire. The
greater a person is, the more and higher his desires and aspi-
rations are. God is so great. He is thoughtful and full of
desire. God's economy is for Him to carry out His desire.

According to the revelation of the Bible, God as the Father,
in the first person of His Godhead, made an economy, a plan,
in eternity past to work out something for His heart's desire.
The Father is altogether related to the divine plan, the divine
economy, the divine arrangement. After the making of such a
plan, God as the Son came in the flesh to be a man for the
purpose of fulfilling the Father's plan to carry out His economy. God as the Father made an economy, and God as the Son
came to accomplish this economy. Then God as the Spirit
applies to us what God as the Son has accomplished. We need
to remember these three simple points—God as the Father
planned, God as the Son accomplished, and God as the Spirit
applies what the Son accomplished. Today we are in the stage
of the Spirit's application. The Spirit's application of what the
Son has accomplished is the function of the Spirit.

The function of the all-inclusive Spirit is His commission.
He has been commissioned by the Godhead in His Trinity to
come to function in applying what God the Son, Christ, has
accomplished according to what God the Father has planned
in His economy. Today we are under the application of the
Third in the Godhead, who carries out what God in the second
person has accomplished according to what God in the first
person has planned in His economy. We have to cover all of this
when we speak about the function of the all-inclusive Spirit.
This brief fellowship covers the entire Bible. The Bible
first shows us God's plan in the person of the Father. Then
the Bible unveils to us God's accomplishment of His plan
in the person of the Second in His Trinity. Then the third
person comes to put everything of the Second's accomplishment
into our experience. This is the function of the all-inclusive
Spirit.

I. CONVICTING SINNERS
TO REPENT AND BELIEVE IN CHRIST

The first function of the all-inclusive Spirit is to convict

John 16 = 8 And when He comes, He will convict the world concerning sin,
and concerning righteousness and concerning judgement.
Christ
Adam
Satan
THE FUNCTIONS OF THE ALL-INCLUSIVE SPIRIT   43

sinners to repent and believe in Christ. This is according to
John 16:7-11. This is a wonderful portion of the Word. Before
going to Russia last year for the spread of the Lord's recovery,
the brothers came to me and we had some fellowship concerning what truths we should bring to the people of Russia. I
proposed that we bring them the seven wonders of the Bible.
John 16:7-11 is included in the wonders of the Bible.

When the Lord Jesus spoke this in John 16, the Spirit of
reality had not yet come. The Lord said that when the Spirit
would come, He would convict the world concerning sin, concerning righteousness, and concerning judgment. When the
Lord Jesus said this, He had not yet gone to the cross to
accomplish redemption. He told His disciples that if He did
not go away, the Comforter, the Spirit of reality, would not
come to them (v. 7). The Son's going was for the coming of the
wonderful Spirit. After dying on the cross, the Son entered
into resurrection. The Spirit of reality came on the day of His
resurrection. This Spirit was breathed by the resurrected
Christ into His disciples to be the reality of whatever Christ
is and whatever Christ has accomplished (John 20:22). After
forty days Christ ascended to the heavens, and ten days later,
on the day of Pentecost, the fulfillment of fifty days, the
Spirit came down as power upon the disciples (Acts 1:8). Such
a Spirit came to convict the world, including all tribes,
tongues, peoples, and nations (Rev. 5:9). This is the third step
of God's economy.

In the economy of God, the first step is the Father's plan-
ning, the second step is the Son's accomplishing, and the third
step is the Spirit's application of Christ's redemption. The
third step is the coming of the Spirit to gain the people whom
God intended to gain. Now in the Spirit's application, the
first step is the convicting of the Spirit. Today our preaching
of the gospel is to carry out the conviction of the Spirit. In
preaching the gospel, we first have to learn to convict people.
We should not merely say good things to people. We have to
carry out the conviction of the Holy Spirit.

When people listen to us, they should be convicted first
concerning righteousness, second concerning sin, and third
concerning judgment. Righteousness is related to Christ, sin

is related to Adam, and judgment is related to Satan. If people do not repent of the sin that is in Adam and believe into Christ as righteousness, they will remain in sin and share the judgment of Satan for eternity (Matt. 25:41). Christ, Adam, and Satan are the three persons which must be involved in our gospel preaching. The function of the all-inclusive Spirit is to convict the fallen people on this earth. Our commission is to convict people. The first step of the Spirit's application is to convict people.

II. SANCTIFYING SINNERS
IN THE PROCESS OF THEIR REPENTANCE
AND THEIR BELIEVING IN CHRIST
BEFORE THEIR REGENERATION

The second function of the all-inclusive Spirit is to sanctify sinners in the process of their repentance and their believing in Christ before their regeneration (1 Pet. 1:2a). To convict people is to sanctify them, and to sanctify them is to separate them. The United States is like a big ocean full of all kinds of fish, all kinds of people, for us to catch, but we do not know how to convict them. We do not know the "high tech" way to preach the gospel. The apostle Paul had many different ways to convict people. Once a man is convicted, he is separated, and to be separated is to be sanctified.

God's sanctification, through His Spirit, of His chosen ones has two sections. The first section is before our repentance and believing, and the second section is after our regeneration. The first section of God the Spirit's sanctification is a part of the convicting. This is the finding work of the woman, signifying the Spirit, in Luke 15:8-9. Many missionaries went to other countries for the purpose of separating people unto Christ, sanctifying them by convicting them. Many of the Chinese were disciples of Confucius before the missionaries went there. Their philosophy, their logic, and their ethical understanding were based on the teachings of Confucius. Eventually, many in the old, conservative country of China were sanctified, separated, from the teachings of Confucius to the gospel of Christ. First Peter 1:2a speaks of the sanctification of people before they believe in Christ. Before people

1 Peter 1:2 Chosen according to the foreknowledge of God the Father in the sanctification of the Spirit ...

believe in Christ they need such a sanctification, such a separation unto Christ.

III. GIVING LIFE TO THE BELIEVING ONES
ALL THE TIME

The Spirit also functions to give life to the believing ones all the time (1 Cor. 15:45b; 2 Cor. 3:6b). While the Spirit is sanctifying the sinners and convicting them, this same Spirit is imparting life into them. We need to consider how the sanctifying, separating, convicting Spirit imparts life to the sinners. While the preachers are preaching the word, the sanctifying, separating, convicting Spirit shows the hearers the beauty of Christ. Spontaneously, there is a kind of aspiration within the hearers to appreciate Christ. Outwardly, the hearers may seem hard, saying that they do not want Jesus. But within, while they are hearing the word, there is an aspiration within them to desire Jesus. This appreciation is the beginning of their faith in Christ.

Thus, life is imparted into them, and that life is a person. Life is Christ (John 14:6a; Col. 3:4a). The beautiful, loving, and attracting Christ as life is imparted into them. Some who hear the gospel may be afraid of their parents and relatives, not daring to confess that they would be a Christian, yet within they have a kind of appreciation of Christ. Through the preaching, they get to know this beautiful Christ. Thus, in their heart faith is produced, and that faith is also Christ. The very life they appreciate is Christ, and even the believing act within them is Christ. At the time they believe, they begin to enjoy the Spirit as the life-giving One.

IV. REGENERATING THE REPENTANT
AND BELIEVING SINNERS

The all-inclusive Spirit regenerates the repentant and believing sinners. This is shown in John 3:5-6. Regeneration is the imparting into us of another life, the divine life, a life other than our human life. D. L. Moody said that regeneration is the greatest miracle in the universe. In an instant a person can become regenerated. He becomes another person, not only with another life but also with another person. The life and the person are one. Christ is His believers' life; Christ is also His believers' person. Before a person is regenerated, he lives merely by his life, by his person. But once he is regenerated, he receives another life, another person. Actually, the person is the life, and the life is the person. Thus, from the time of our regeneration, it is no longer we that live, but another person, Christ, lives in us (Gal. 2:20a). Now Christ is within us as our life.

V. SANCTIFYING AFTER THE BELIEVERS' REGENERATION

After regeneration, the second section of sanctifying begins. We are regenerated, but we are still full of our natural peculiarity. Therefore, the Spirit functions to sanctify the believers after their regeneration (Rom. 6:19, 22; 15:16). This sanctification involves a transformation from the natural disposition to a spiritual one by Christ as the life-giving Spirit saturating all the inward parts of our being with God's nature of holiness.

VI. RENEWING THE BELIEVERS

Because of our oldness, we all need to be renewed. The all-inclusive Spirit renews us (Titus 3:5). We are renewed first in our spirit and then in our soul, including our mind, emotion, and will. All the inward parts of our being have to be renewed. We should not think, feel, or decide according to our old, natural man. We are Christians, so we should be renewed in everything. Even in the way that we comb our hair, we need to be renewed. In the way that we keep and arrange our rooms, we need to be renewed. In selecting a pair of shoes and in shining our shoes, we need to be renewed. Everything in our life should bear a sign that we are God's children, because we are renewed. We need to be renewed in our thinking, in our loving and hating, in our deciding, and in everything.

VII. TRANSFORMING THE BELIEVERS

The Spirit also functions to transform the believers (2 Cor. 3:18). We need to be transformed from one form to another form. A mere outward change is not transformation. Transformation

is a metabolic change within by the addition of a new element.
Confucius taught renewing too, but his kind of renewing was
outward without any new element added. Morticians use cos-
metics to make the faces of corpses look colorful outwardly,
but this is not transformation. When we are nourished with
organic food, this nourishing carries out a kind of metabolic
transformation within us to give us a healthy appearance.
Transformation is a metabolic change.

I hope that all of us would change in a metabolic way. We
should be beautiful metabolically in an organic transformation. The word *transformed* is used only two times in the New
Testament—in 2 Corinthians 3:18 and in Romans 12:2. Second
Corinthians 3:18 says that we are being transformed from
glory to glory, even as from the Lord Spirit. The Spirit with
the Lord as the element changes our being metabolically to
accomplish transformation in us. Romans 12:2 charges us not
to be fashioned according to this age but to be transformed by
the renewing of the mind. I would encourage us to study
these wonderful verses with the help of the notes in the
Recovery Version. If you read 2 Corinthians 3:18 plus Romans
12:2 with all the notes, you will receive much help. We all
need to experience the transforming Spirit.

VIII. SEALING THE BELIEVERS

Ephesians 1:13 shows us that the Spirit functions to seal
the believers. The seal needs the sealing ink. When a piece of
paper is sealed, the sealing ink saturates the paper. Then the
sealed paper bears the appearance, the image, of the seal.
Furthermore, the sealing transfuses the element of the ink
into the paper. Then the sealing ink and the paper are mingled together as one.

The sealing of the Spirit is a fine point of the function of
the all-inclusive Spirit. The Holy Spirit today is on us as a seal
and is continually sealing us. We are like the paper absorbing
the sealing element of the Holy Spirit as the seal into us.
Because we have been sealed, we bear a mark indicating that
we belong to our God, that we are God's inheritance. When we
put our seal upon a book, that seal indicates that the book is

ours. God put His Spirit as His seal upon us, indicating that we are His possession.

IX. PLEDGING IN THE BELIEVERS

The Spirit also functions as a pledge within the believers (Eph. 1:14; 2 Cor. 1:22b). A pledge is a guarantee. The Spirit as the pledge within us guarantees that God is our inheritance. The sealing indicates that we are God's inheritance, and the pledging guarantees that God is our inheritance. This is clearly revealed in Ephesians 1:13-14. The crucial word in verse 13 is *sealed,* and the crucial word in verse 14 is *pledge.*

X. INDWELLING THE BELIEVERS

The all-inclusive Spirit is indwelling the believers (Rom. 8:11). The Spirit not only dwells within us but also indwells us. To indwell is to make home, or reside (cf. Eph. 3:17). Today the Spirit is within us, and He is functioning to indwell us.

All of the functions of the all-inclusive Spirit are very mysterious and abstract. In each believer all these functions are acting day by day. The world does not see this, but we believers can realize the functions of the Spirit. This is because these functions are actions. The Spirit is moving within us every day, even every moment.

XI. LEADING THE BELIEVERS

This indwelling Spirit is the leading Spirit. He leads the believers (Rom. 8:14; Gal. 5:18). Romans 8:14 says that as many as are led by the Spirit of God, these are sons of God. We are the sons of God because we have a particular Guide, who leads us always in a particular way. Whatever the Spirit tells us in His leading of us is true. We have to listen to Him.

But because I speak the truth, you do not believe Me.

XII. WITNESSING

The Spirit also functions in witnessing, or testifying. First, He witnesses concerning Christ (John 15:26; 1 John 5:6). While the gospel preaching is going on, the Spirit is always working within the listeners in the way of witnessing. This is why many unbelievers wonder why certain preachers are so convincing. Actually, it is not they who are convincing. While they are speaking, another One, a witnessing person, the witnessing Spirit, is working in the listeners. Actually, the witnessing Spirit within the listeners speaks more than the speaker who is witnessing concerning Christ. Otherwise, how could people such as the conservative Chinese ever believe in Jesus? Logically speaking, this is impossible. But whenever a witness of Christ is speaking about Christ, another Witness, the Spirit, works to witness concerning Christ within the listeners.

Also, the Spirit witnesses with the spirit of the believers that they are children of God (Rom. 8:16). How do we know we are children of God? We know because there is an inner witnessing, and that witnessing is the witnessing Spirit with our spirit. The two spirits work together. Some who become fallen or defeated in their Christian life may go to a sinful place. But when they go, there is a checking within them which says, "Should a child of God be here?" The witnessing Spirit with our spirit is witnessing all the time, but many Christians are not used to listening to this inward witness. When we go shopping, there is always an inward checking, an inward witnessing, telling us that certain things are not what children of God should buy. In everything we do, we have the witnessing Spirit functioning within us.

XIII. BEING THE REALITY OF CHRIST

The Spirit is the reality of Christ (John 15:26; 1 John 5:6). The Spirit is the reality of Christ's death, the reality of Christ's resurrection, and the reality of all the divine attributes of Christ. If you have the Spirit, you have Christ's humility and Christ's love. The reality of everything that Christ is, everything that Christ has, and even everything that Christ has accomplished is the Spirit.

XIV. COMFORTING THE CHURCHES

Acts 9:31 says that the church went on in the comfort of the Holy Spirit. The churches were not only comforted but also were in the comfort of the Spirit. The word *comfort* in the Bible implies satisfaction, rest, and enlightenment. If you are satisfied, your thirst is quenched and you have rest. Also, you are not in darkness. No one in darkness can be comforted. Darkness itself is a trouble. When light is here, we are comforted. When light is gone, we are troubled. The church needs the comfort of the Spirit, which includes satisfaction, rest, and enlightenment.

XV. BEING THE JOY IN THE BELIEVERS FOR THE KINGDOM OF GOD

The all-inclusive Spirit is the joy in the believers for the kingdom of God (Rom. 14:17; Acts 13:52). Romans 14:17 says that the kingdom of God is righteousness, peace, and joy in the Holy Spirit. Acts 13:52 says that the disciples were filled with joy and with the Holy Spirit. Thus, one of the functions of the Spirit is to make us joyful. He is our joy.

The above fifteen items should give us a view of the functions of the Spirit. They show us how the Spirit functions to apply to us what Christ is, what Christ has, what Christ has accomplished, and even what Christ will do. In other words, the functioning Spirit is making the Triune God in what He is, what He has, what He has accomplished, and what He will accomplish, one with us. Thus, the Christian life is a life by the all-inclusive Spirit.

Southern Baptist: forbid talking about the Spirit.

CHAPTER FIVE

THE FUNCTIONS
OF THE ALL-INCLUSIVE SPIRIT

(2)

Scripture Reading: Eph. 3:16; Phil. 1:19b; 1 Cor. 12:4, 7-11;
Acts 6:3, 5; 7:55; 11:24; 13:52; 2:4a; 4:31; 9:17; 13:9; Matt.
12:28; Eph. 4:3-4a; 1 Cor. 2:10; Rom. 8:13b, 11; 1 Cor. 6:17; Gal.
5:16, 25, 22-23; 6:8b; 2 Cor. 13:14; Eph. 4:4, 16; Rev. 2:7, 11, 17,
29; 3:6, 13, 22; 4:5b; 5:6b; 22:17a

In this message we want to continue our fellowship concerning the functions of the all-inclusive Spirit. In the previous
message we saw fifteen of these functions, and in this message we will see twenty more. The Spirit, although abstract
and hidden, is mentioned frequently in the Bible. But, sorry,
many of those in fundamental Christianity do not see this
clearly.

In the previous message and in this message, we are point-
ing out thirty-five functions of the all-inclusive Spirit. These
are only some of the many functions of the Spirit. Revelation 22
shows us the throne of God and of the Lamb with the Spirit as
the river of water of life proceeding out of it (v. 1).

God and the Lamb are sitting on the throne. We may
wonder how one throne can seat two people. In Revelation 21
and 22 in the description of the New Jerusalem, we can find
the explanation. Revelation 21:23 says that the lamp in the
New Jerusalem is the Lamb. The Lamb is the lamp, and God
is the light within the lamp (22:5). The Lamb as the lamp is
the One sitting on the throne with God as the light within
Him. The one throne for both God and the Lamb indicates
that God and the Lamb are one.

In NJ, light signifies the Father.
lamp & lamb signifies the Son
the river of water of life proceeding out of the throne signifies the Spirit.

52 THE CHRISTIAN LIFE

From this One, flows the river of water of life. Revelation 21 and 22 present the ultimate, consummated revelation of the New Jerusalem. In this presentation we can see the Father, the Son—Christ, and the Spirit. The light is a figure signifying the Father (Rev. 22:5). The word *Christ* is not mentioned in these chapters, but Christ is revealed as the Lamb and as the lamp. The Lamb and the lamp are not physical things, but figures, signifying the Son of God, Christ. Then there is a river. This river is not a physical river but a figure signifying the Spirit.

The flowing of the river is the top function, the total function, of the Spirit. The flowing of the river quenches the thirst of the whole city, supplying the whole city with the spiritual water of life. Thus, quenching is another function of the Spirit. The quenching of the Spirit is saturating, the saturating is transfusing, and the transfusing is infusing. These are more functions of the Spirit. Revelation 22 also reveals that the river grows the tree of life. According to Revelation 22, the tree of life does not grow in earth but in water. It is the water that grows the tree of life. This is another function of the Spirit. There are many functions of the Spirit revealed throughout the entire Bible.

The entire Bible is a book on the Spirit and a book of the Spirit. Genesis 1:1 says, "In the beginning God...." God here is *Elohim* in Hebrew, a plural word. Thus, the first verse of the Bible refers to the Triune God. Then the second verse refers to the Spirit of God, saying that the Spirit of God brooded over the face of the waters. Then at the end of the Bible in Revelation 22:17 there are the Spirit and the bride.

The Spirit of God is one aspect, and the Spirit with the bride is another aspect. The Spirit of God was the Spirit not yet consummated. The unconsummated Spirit of God was not yet ready for marriage. But at the end of the Bible, there are the Spirit and the bride. This means that the Spirit is married. In Revelation 22, He is the consummated Spirit as the Bridegroom. The bride needs a bridegroom. The Groom is the consummated Spirit, and the consummated Spirit is the consummated Triune God.

Actually, the revelation of the all-inclusive Spirit and the functions of this Spirit are endless. What I am doing in these messages is giving us a little view to know what the Spirit is doing. Actually, we cannot exhaust the functions of the all-inclusive Spirit.

XVI. STRENGTHENING THE BELIEVERS

The Spirit functions to strengthen the believers. In Ephesians 3:16 Paul prayed that the Father would grant the saints "to be strengthened with power through His Spirit into the inner man." The Father strengthens us through the Spirit. Thus, the means that the Father uses to strengthen us is the Spirit. For Christ to make His home in our hearts, there is the need of strengthening. No one can do this but the Spirit of God. In Ephesians 3 the Spirit of God is the strengthening Spirit. The Spirit not only quenches, saturates, transfuses, infuses, and grows, but also strengthens.

XVII. SUPPLYING THE BELIEVERS

We know that the Spirit functions to supply the believers because Philippians 1:19 speaks of "the bountiful supply of the Spirit of Jesus Christ." The Spirit of God had to be processed and consummated to be the Spirit of Jesus Christ.

In eternity past the Triune God possessed merely divinity. In this sense, we may say that He was "raw," or unprocessed. Then He created the universe and a man by the name of Adam with the intention of coming into him. After the creation of man, however, man became fallen. Later, the Triune God came to join Himself with humanity. He became a man who was both divine and human. He lived on this earth in humanity for thirty-three and a half years. After having passed through such a human living, He was qualified to die an all-inclusive death. In order to die such an all-inclusive death, He had to be a God-man, a man mingled with God, and He had to pass through human life for thirty-three and a half years. Without such a qualification, He would not have been able to die such a wonderful death.

He entered into this death and stayed in death for three days. Then He walked out of death into resurrection to become a life-giving Spirit (1 Cor. 15:45b). This life-giving Spirit now consists of divinity, humanity, human living, Christ's all-inclusive death, and His wonderful resurrection. The life-giving Spirit is the issue of the Triune God's process from incarnation to resurrection. Now this life-giving Spirit is not merely the Spirit of God but the Spirit of Jesus Christ. With such a Spirit, there is the bountiful supply.

Lemon tea can be used as an illustration of the bountiful Spirit. First, there is only the plain water. But when tea and lemon are added to the water, it becomes a composition of three elements. When we drink it, we receive the elements of the water, the tea, and the lemon. This can be considered as a "bountiful-supply drink." The Spirit of Jesus Christ is such an all-inclusive bountiful drink, with all the elements of the Triune God's person and processes to supply us.

The Spirit not only strengthens us but also supplies us. It is difficult to explain how the Spirit strengthens and supplies us. When we eat food, we are strengthened and supplied, but it is difficult to say how this takes place. Even medical doctors cannot explain fully what it means to be nourished. Many years ago no one knew what vitamins were. There was not even such a word in the dictionary years ago. Our ancestors, however, were nourished with many vitamins without knowing about vitamins.

We may feel fatigued at a certain point in the day, but after we eat, we are nourished, strengthened, and supplied. We may not be able to explain how this happens, but we can experience and enjoy it. In the same way, we may not be able to explain how the Spirit strengthens and supplies us, but we can experience His strengthening and supplying.

Some of us may come to the meetings in a fatigued way. We need to get ourselves nourished, strengthened, and supplied by eating a "meal," by enjoying the all-inclusive Spirit. For us to eat a physical meal may require twenty-five to thirty minutes. But to take a spiritual meal, we may need just two and a half minutes. When we take a few minutes to pray, we are strengthened and supplied by the functioning Spirit.

If the spiritual eating (praying → got strengthen) is superstitious, then our physical eating is also superstitious.

XVIII. DISTRIBUTING THE GIFTS TO THE BELIEVERS

The Spirit also distributes the gifts to the believers (1 Cor. 12:4, 7-11). In order to receive the gifts for service, we need to contact the Spirit through prayer every day. We do not need to know what kinds of gifts, abilities or capacities for service, we will receive. If we pray and contact the Spirit, He will distribute gifts to us. We may not know what these gifts are, but when we come to the church meetings, we will function with a particular capacity. With our physical being, we have a walking capacity and a speaking capacity which come out of our human life. After much praying to contact the Spirit, we will receive some spiritual capacity; that capacity becomes a gift, and that gift brings in a kind of function.

XIX. FILLING THE BELIEVERS INWARDLY

The all-inclusive Spirit fills the believers inwardly (Acts 6:3, 5; 7:55; 11:24; 13:52). Before I come to speak, I need to ask the Lord to fill me up with Himself as the Spirit. Without the filling up of the Spirit, the *pneuma*, we will be like a flat tire. We can experience being filled with the Spirit inwardly by spending time with the Lord in prayer.

XX. FILLING THE BELIEVERS OUTWARDLY

The all-inclusive Spirit also fills the believers outwardly (Acts 2:4a; 4:31; 9:17; 13:9). The Spirit's outward filling is the outpouring of the Spirit. On the day of Pentecost, the Spirit was poured out. Fifty days before that time, on the day of resurrection, the Lord Jesus came to the disciples to breathe the Spirit into them (John 20:22). Then the Spirit became the inward Spirit. On the day of resurrection, He breathed the Spirit into the disciples as the *pneuma*, as the breath, as the Spirit of life. Then fifty days later, the ascended Lord poured out the Spirit upon the believers as the Spirit of power. The Spirit of life is the essential Spirit for our life and living. The Spirit poured out upon us is the economical Spirit for our move and work. The economical Spirit is for our authority to accomplish a work according to God's economy.

XXI. CASTING OUT THE DEMONS

In Matthew 12:28 the Lord said that He cast out demons by the Spirit of God. We need to realize that demons and demon possession are real. About one hundred years ago, a Presbyterian missionary from the United States by the name of Dr. Nevius went to China. He wrote a book entitled *Demon Possession and Allied Themes,* in which he told story after story of cases involving demon possession.

Today in the United States, it is difficult to see a real case of demon possession. What the Pentecostals say concerning demon possession is not trustworthy. Their so-called cases of demon possession are actually cases of mental illness.

In 1948 I was in Nanking, China. There was a boy there who suddenly became crazy. Some of the saints considered that he was demon-possessed. They came together to pray to cast out the "demon," but the more they prayed, the more he was active. Then they wondered about this situation. It seemed to them that the Lord's name was not that powerful or mighty. They prayed in the name of the Lord Jesus for the "demon" to depart, but it did not work. Then they referred the case to me and told me what had happened. I told them that this was not a case of demon possession, but a case of mental illness. I told these saints that this boy should be sent to the hospital for a period of time to be under some medical care. Eventually, the boy was admitted to the hospital, and he became well.

Today, cases of demon possession occur mostly in backward countries which are very primitive and poor. Many people in these backward countries do not have much education or knowledge. They are very poor and under all kinds of depression. The demons can have the opportunity to possess such persons. In modern countries many people are educated, so the opportunity for the demons to possess people is rare. Modern countries, however, are full of people with mental illness. Too much knowledge and education can be a factor of mental illness. In the primitive countries, there are more cases of physical demon possession, but in the educated countries, there are more people with psychological problems. At any rate, the Spirit is the means by which the demons can be cast out.

Once you know the knowledge, it cannot be reduced.

Too much knowledge → divorce mental illness. They need the Spirit.

XXII. ONENESS-KEEPING WITHIN THE BELIEVERS
for THE BODY OF CHRIST

Eph 4:12 Perfecting of the saints unto the work of the ministry, unto the building
The Spirit functions in oneness-keeping within the believ-
ers for the Body of Christ (Eph. 4:3-4a). We need to be diligent
to keep the oneness of the Spirit, which is the oneness of the
Body. When we exercise to keep the oneness, the Spirit within
us keeps the oneness. *Eph 4:16 ... & being joined together and being knit together thru every joint of the riches supply, and through the operation in the measure of each one part, causes the growth of the Body unto the building up of itself in love.*

Most, if not all, of the teachings in Christianity today do
not touch this line of the all-inclusive Spirit with His functions. The teachings are mostly ethical and are concerning
man's physical or psychological welfare. People teach that if
a person is a good Christian, he will have peace within and
without; he will be blessed to have a good marriage life and a
good family life. This is according to the human, natural concept. It is difficult to find anyone teaching about Christ's
making His home in our hearts.

Who in Christianity sees or speaks of the organic Body of
Christ? The better teachers say that Christ died for our sins,
so now we have to believe in Him. They say that because of
His death on the cross, God forgives us of our sins, so one day
we will go to heaven. They cover this but nothing further. But
when we speak concerning Christ and the church revealed
and typified in the Psalms, very few of those in Christianity
would have any interest in this. *We're not talking the way of socialsing,*

I am saying this to show us that in comparison with today's *the way*
Christianity, we are on another planet, a "Christ planet." I *of rock*
have considered in the past that our rate of increase has been *music,*
too low. As I was spending time with the Lord recently, He *but the*
touched my understanding in this matter. We have to realize *way of*
that the way we take in following the Lord cannot have a high *Christ,*
rate of increase. The way we are taking is really a narrow *the way*
way. The messages given in this ministry are altogether in *of the*
another category, on another planet. *Spirit.*

Other groups of Christians use natural and worldly ways
to attract people. They use the ways of being social, of rock
music, and of choirs with colorful robes. They use these ways
to gain people, but we cannot use these ways. When people
get saved and come into our meeting, they hear the pure word
of God. We shared recently that the goal of Psalm 8 is to join

the earth to the heavens and to bring down the heavens to the earth, making the earth and the heavens one. Someone hearing this may wonder what this has to do with his personal benefit and self-interest. But in our ministry we do not speak much concerning man's personal benefit. We speak and have spoken Christ in every message year after year. I am so thankful to the Lord that many of us in His recovery are still eager to hear the things concerning Christ as the centrality and universality of God's economy for His heart's desire. I say again that this teaching is on another planet. Because of this, we cannot expect to have too high a rate in our increase.

XXIII. REVEALING THE DEPTHS OF GOD TO THE BELIEVERS

The Spirit reveals the depths of God to the believers (1 Cor. 2:10). Every bit of the depths of God is Christ. Christ is so deep, and the contents, the very constituents, of our messages are concerning Christ.

In 1 Corinthians 1, Paul taught that Christ is God's power and God's wisdom (v. 24). Christ is wisdom to us from God as our righteousness, as our sanctification, and as our redemption (v. 30). These aspects of Christ are the depths of God. As the Spirit reveals the depths of God, Christ, to us, we are renewed, sanctified, transformed, conformed, and glorified. Only the Spirit can reveal the depths of God to us.

XXIV. APPLYING THE DEATH OF CHRIST TO THE BELIEVERS

The Spirit applies the death of Christ to the believers (Rom. 8:13b). When I was a young Christian, I heard that according to the Bible, I had been crucified with Christ (Gal. 2:20a). But I wondered how I could have been crucified with Christ. Spacewise He was in Palestine, and timewise He died nearly two thousand years ago. I could not figure out how I could have been crucified with Him at the same time. Later I realized that when Christ was crucified, according to God's economy we were included in Him. This is an accomplished fact.

I still did not know, however, how to experience the death of Christ. I was told that I had to reckon myself as having been crucified with Christ according to Paul's word in Romans 6:11, but reckoning did not work. The more I reckoned myself as having died with Christ, the more I seemed to be alive. Eventually, Brother Watchman Nee came to the conclusion that the very death revealed in Romans 6 can be applied only by the Spirit in Romans 8. Romans 8:13b says, "If by the Spirit you put to death the practices of the body, you will live." This means the Spirit applies Christ's death to the practices of our mortal body. The Spirit indwelling us works to apply the death of Christ as the killing element to kill all the practices of our troublesome body. Reckoning does not work, but the application of the Spirit works.

XXV. APPLYING THE RESURRECTION OF CHRIST TO THE BELIEVERS

The all-inclusive Spirit applies the resurrection of Christ to the believers (Rom. 8:11). In order to enjoy the application of the resurrection of Christ by the Spirit, you need to be revived every morning. If you practice this every day, I must tell you that ten or twenty minutes actually are not adequate. You need a longer time. You may say that since you are working, you cannot spare that much time. On the one hand, I agree with you, but on the other hand, you should still try your best to spend more time with the Lord in the morning. According to my experience, I need a longer time. If I spend a longer time in morning revival contacting the Lord in fellowship with Him for thirty minutes, forty-five minutes, or even an hour, I am more fully in the enjoyment of Christ's resurrection.

Being in resurrection brings us many benefits. In resurrection we have peace, joy, rest, strength, and everything positive. The Spirit is the totality of resurrection. Furthermore, the resurrection can be applied to us only by the life-giving Spirit, by the Spirit of Jesus Christ. The reality of resurrection can be ours only through the applying Spirit. This is a great function of the all-inclusive Spirit.

XXVI. MINGLING WITH THE SPIRIT OF THE BELIEVERS, MAKING THE TWO ONE SPIRIT

The all-inclusive Spirit of God mingles with the spirit of the believers, making the two one spirit (1 Cor. 6:17). Our spirit has been regenerated by the Spirit of God (John 3:6), who is now in us (1 Cor. 6:19) and is one with our spirit (Rom. 8:16).

XXVII. BEING THE ESSENCE OF THE DIVINE LIFE BY WHICH THE BELIEVERS LIVE AND WALK

The Spirit is the essence of the divine life by which the believers live and walk. The divine life, essentially speaking, is the Spirit. Galatians 5:16 and 25 both refer to our living and walking by the Spirit as the essence of the divine life.

XXVIII. BRINGING FORTH THE FRUIT OF THE VIRTUES OF THE BELIEVERS

The Spirit brings forth the fruit of the virtues of the believers (Gal. 5:22-23). We believers need virtues, but not according to our natural character and conduct. We need the fruit of Christian virtues borne by the Spirit. The Spirit moves and lives in us to bear fruit, the fruit of Christian virtues. These are not the natural virtues but the virtues of Christ expressed in our spiritual life.

XXIX. BEING THE AIM OF THE BELIEVERS' SOWING

The Spirit is the aim of the believers' sowing (Gal. 6:8b). Whatever we do is a kind of sowing. If we hate people, we sow the seed of hatred unto the flesh. Then we will reap hatred from others. We should not sow unto the flesh but unto the Spirit. To sow unto the Spirit is to sow for the Spirit, with the desire and aim of the Spirit in view, to accomplish what the Spirit desires.

XXX. CIRCULATING, IN HIS FELLOWSHIP, GOD THE FATHER'S LOVE AND CHRIST THE SON'S GRACE WITHIN THE BELIEVERS FOR THEIR ENJOYMENT

The Spirit circulates within the believers in His fellowship. He does not circulate rumors or today's news. He circulates

God the Father's love and Christ the Son's grace within us for our enjoyment (2 Cor. 13:14). This circulating is the fellowship of the Spirit. The love of God through the grace of Christ is circulated by the Spirit's fellowship for our enjoyment.

XXXI. BEING THE ESSENCE FOR THE ORGANIC BUILDING UP OF THE BODY OF CHRIST

The Spirit is the essence for the organic building up of the Body of Christ (Eph. 4:4, 16). The organic building up of the Body of Christ is altogether the total function of the Spirit in all of us. Ephesians 4:4a says, "One Body and one Spirit." Verse 12 speaks of the perfecting of the saints. Verse 15 speaks of our growth in life. Then verse 16 reveals the Spirit in the Body building up the Body through every member, that is, through each one part of the Body and through every joint of the supply. All of this is involved with the function of the Spirit.

The Spirit moves in one member to produce one kind of function and within another member to produce another kind of function. The Spirit produces many kinds of functions in the Body. Every part operates in its measure, and all the joints of supply do their work as the issue of the functioning of the all-inclusive Spirit. This is why I say that there are many, many functions of the all-inclusive Spirit. Without such a Spirit, the Body of Christ could not be organically built up.

XXXII. SPEAKING AS THE LORD

The Spirit speaks as the Lord. In Revelation 2 and 3, at the beginning of each of the seven epistles it is the Lord who speaks (2:1, 8, 12, 18; 3:1, 7, 14), but at the end of each epistle it is the Spirit who speaks to the churches (2:7, 11, 17, 29; 3:6, 13, 22). Thus, the Spirit is one with the Lord in speaking, speaking as the Lord. Speaking is a great function of the all-inclusive Spirit.

XXXIII. SHINING AND BURNING AS THE SEVEN LAMPS OF FIRE BEFORE GOD'S THRONE

The Spirit shines and burns as the seven lamps of fire before God's throne (Rev. 4:5b). The seven lamps of fire being

before God's throne means that the fire in the lamps is shining and burning to carry out God's divine and spiritual
administration.

XXXIV. OBSERVING AND TRANSFUSING
AS THE SEVEN EYES OF GOD

The Spirit is observing and transfusing as the seven eyes
of God (Rev. 5:6b). The Spirit as the seven lamps of fire is also
the seven eyes of God, of Christ. Christ looks at us with His
eyes to observe us, and when He observes us, He transfuses
Himself into us with all of His feelings and sentiment. This is
the Spirit's function. When we look at the Lord, allowing Him
to look at us, He observes us and transfuses us with what He
intends to say or to do.

XXXV. SPEAKING WITH THE CHURCH AS THE BRIDE

The all-inclusive Spirit speaks with the church as the
bride (Rev. 22:17a). The consummated Spirit of God, who is
the consummated God, becomes the Bridegroom to marry
the bride, the church. This marriage is a union between the
processed and consummated Triune God and the transformed
and glorified tripartite man. The processed and consummated
Triune God and the church as the bride become a universal
couple.

In Revelation 2 and 3, it was the Spirit speaking to the
churches. At the end of Revelation, it is the Spirit and the bride,
the church, speaking together as one. This indicates that the
church's experience of the Spirit has improved to the extent
that she has become one with the Spirit, who is the ultimate
consummation of the Triune God.

THE ALL-INCLUSIVE DEATH OF CHRIST

Scripture Reading: Rom. 5:12; 1 Cor. 15:22a; Heb. 9:27; Rom. 5:10; 2 Cor. 5:14-15; Heb. 9:26; Rom. 8:3b; Heb. 9:28; 1 Cor. 15:3; Matt. 26:28; John 1:29; Heb. 2:14; John 12:31; Gal. 6:14; Col. 2:15; Rom. 6:6a; Gal. 6:14-15; 2 Cor. 4:10a, 11a, 12a, 16a; Gal. 5:24; Rom. 6:6b; Eph. 2:15; Col. 2:14; Eph. 2:16; John 12:24; Rom. 12:5; 1 Cor. 10:17; John 19:34

In the Scripture reading for this message, we have listed thirty-two verses. All these verses are like the pieces of a jigsaw puzzle concerning the revelation of the all-inclusive death of Christ. These verses are scattered throughout the Bible. Under the inspiration of the Spirit, the Bible was written in this way. The truths are scattered here and there throughout the Bible. Time, insight, and skill are needed to put these pieces of the truth together. Then we can have a complete picture. In this message we want to put the pieces of the truth concerning Christ's all-inclusive death together, so that we can have a complete picture of His death.

In the early days, by reading some spiritual books, I found out that Christ's death has two aspects—the objective aspect and the subjective aspect. The objective aspect is that Christ died for my sins (1 Cor. 15:3), and the subjective aspect is that when Christ was crucified, I was crucified with Him (Gal. 2:20a). Through my reading of the Bible for over sixty years, I have collected the scattered pieces of the truth concerning the all-inclusive death of Christ.

The Bible was not written in a systematic way according to our thought. It was written according to what Isaiah said in Isaiah 28:13: "Therefore Jehovah's word to them will be: / Rule upon rule, rule upon rule; / Line upon line, line upon

line; / Here a little, there a little." We need the sight and the
insight to put all the pieces of a certain truth together. I have
spent much time to put the pieces of the truth concerning
Christ's death together. All the verses I have collected from
the Scripture give us a marvelous picture of Christ's wonderful, excellent, and all-inclusive death.

If we do not know the all-inclusive death of Christ, and if
we do not experience His death in our daily life, we cannot
live the Christian life. Without experiencing His death, we
can live at best only an ethical life. We may live an ethical life
according to our culture in the Chinese way or in the American
way. Ethics are always different from country to country.
We may live a life which is good in the eyes of people, but
such a living has altogether nothing to do with the Christian
life.

The Christian life is to live Christ, but to live Christ, we
must die. If you do not know that you have been crucified
before you were born, you can never live the Christian life. We
have to realize that not only many negative things but also
many of our natural positive things need to be dealt with sub-
jectively by the cross of Christ. For example, we may always
gossip about others. Some saints are the "information desk
of the church." If people come to this "desk," they can find out
all the information about the saints in the church. This is
negative. Things like this need to be dealt with by the cross
because they are of the flesh. And the good things, the ethical
things, which are by our natural life, even though they are
positive, also need to be dealt with by the cross of Christ
because they are not something by Christ and cannot be considered something of the Christian life. In order to live the
Christian life, we must be under the killing of the cross of
Christ in the subjective experience of His all-inclusive death.

I. THE DEATH OF CHRIST BEING DIFFERENT
FROM THE DEATH OF ADAM

The death of Christ is different from the death of Adam.
The death of Adam brings every one of us into death, making
all of us dead.

A. The Death of Adam
Having Come In through Sin

The death of Adam came in through sin, and all men have suffered of his death (Rom. 5:12; 1 Cor. 15:22a; Heb. 9:27). Even before Adam's sin, death was mentioned in Genesis. God warned Adam that if he partook of the tree of the knowledge of good and evil, he would surely die (Gen. 2:17). After God created man, He put him in a garden before two trees: the tree of life and the tree of the knowledge of good and evil. The Bible does not say that there is a tree called the tree of death. The tree of death is called the tree of the knowledge of good and evil. On the positive side, there is a tree called the tree of life. On the negative side, there is a tree which we would think should be called the tree of death. But the Bible calls the tree of death "the tree of the knowledge of good and evil." Knowledge plus good plus evil equals death.

Today if you are trying to collect knowledge or do good, you are involved with the element of death. We would always consider evil as death, but we would not consider knowledge or good as death. The knowledge such as the knowledge concerning Christ and the church is positive, but the knowledge that has nothing to do with the reality of God's economy is negative, being in the same category of good and evil, which are of death.

We should not think that death was not present before Adam's fall. Before Adam's fall, death was there with Satan. Hebrews 2:14 says that the devil is the one who has the might of death. Death is Satan's might. Satan is the very source of death, just as God is the very source of life. God has authority.

In his cleverness Satan contacted the female first. Through the female he reached Adam, and Adam took in Satan's proposal. When you take in another's proposal, that means you take the proposer. Thus, the proposer got into Adam. The result of Adam's fall was death. Thus, Romans 5:12 tells us very clearly that sin entered into the world, into the human race, through one man, Adam. Then this sin brought in death as the result, the end. The death of Adam is altogether negative. Adam's death caused all of us, his descendants, to be in death. We were born not only in sin but also in death. Sin and death were our inheritance at our birth.

B. The Death of Christ Coming to His Believers through His Redemption

The death of Christ comes to His believers through His redemption, and all His believers have been redeemed that they may enjoy the salvation of His life (Rom. 5:10; 2 Cor. 5:14-15). Christ accomplished redemption on the cross. His death was a redeeming death. A positive, wonderful, good, and excellent death has come to us. If we reject this death, we will suffer the negative death in Adam.

The purpose of Christ's death is not that we may go to heaven. Even the heavens have been redeemed by Christ's death. Colossians 1:20 says that Christ's death has reconciled all things, including the things in the heavens. Satan's rebellion contaminated also the heavens, so even the heavens needed to be reconciled to God. Reconciliation is for the enemy, so all the created things, including the heavens, were enemies to God. Through His redeeming death, Christ reconciled all things to Himself. All His believers have been redeemed that they may enjoy the salvation of His life. Adam's death brought us into death. Christ's death, however, brought us into life.

II. THE DEATH OF CHRIST BEING THE REDEEMING AND LIFE-RELEASING AND LIFE-IMPARTING DEATH

The death of Christ is the redeeming and life-releasing and life-imparting death. The redeeming death is on the negative side. The life-releasing and life-imparting death is on the positive side. Hence, Christ's death is all-inclusive.

A. On the Negative Side

The redeeming death of Christ is on the negative side.

1. Dealing with Sin

Christ's death dealt with sin. There are three aspects to His dealing with sin.

a. To Put Away Sin in Our Nature

Christ dealt with sin in His death to put away sin in our nature (Heb. 9:26; Rom. 8:3b). Men are sinners because sin is in their nature. A fruit tree does not learn how to bring forth fruits. It brings forth fruits spontaneously out of its nature. Similarly, men always lie because sin is in their nature. There is not a trade school teaching people how to lie. Parents may warn their children not to lie, but the children lie spontaneously in many ways. Children do not learn to lie. They were born to lie because sin is within them.

Hebrews 9:26 says that Christ "has been manifested for the putting away of sin through the sacrifice of Himself." This refers to the putting away of sin in our nature. Then Romans 8:3 says that Christ, in His death on the cross, "condemned sin in the flesh." When Christ became flesh, according to Romans 8:3, He was in the likeness of the flesh of sin, but He did not have the sin of the flesh (2 Cor. 5:21; Heb. 4:15). But our flesh is the flesh of sin. Our flesh is constituted with sin. It is a sinful flesh. Through Christ's crucifixion in the flesh, God condemned sin, which was brought by Satan into man's flesh, into man's nature.

b. To Bear Our Sins

Christ died on the cross to bear our sins (Heb. 9:28; 1 Cor. 15:3; Matt. 26:28). These are the sins in our conduct, in our behavior, not in our nature. Hebrews 9:26 speaks of Christ's death dealing with the sin in our nature, whereas verse 28 speaks of His death dealing with the sins in our conduct, in our behavior. First Corinthians 15:3 says that Christ died for our sins, and Matthew 26:28 says that His blood was shed for the forgiveness of sins.

c. To Take Away Sin
in Totality

John 1:29 says, "Behold, the Lamb of God, who takes away the sin of the world!" This refers to sin in its totality. Christ died to take away sin in totality.

When we define the death of Christ in dealing with sin, we have to cover the above three items with all the related Scripture references.

2. Dealing with Satan

The death of Christ, on the negative side, also dealt with Satan.

a. To Destroy the Devil, Who Has the Might of Death

Christ's death destroyed the devil, who has the might of death (Heb. 2:14). Satan is the source of death who has the might of death.

b. To Judge the World and to Cast Out the Ruler of the World

Through His death on the cross, Christ judged the world of Satan and cast out Satan as the ruler of the world (John 12:31; Gal. 6:14). The world belongs to Satan. It is Satan's kingdom and Satan's possession. Christ's death on the cross judged the satanic world and cast out Satan as the ruler of the world.

c. To Strip Off the Rulers and the Authorities of the Rebellious Angels

Colossians 2:15 says, "Stripping off the rulers and the authorities, He made a display of them openly, triumphing over them in it." This is a very deep verse concerning the death of Christ. While Christ was dying on the cross, He did a work to strip off the evil angelic rulers and authorities of the rebellious angels, and made a display of them openly, triumphing over them in the cross.

When Christ was being crucified on the cross, there was a visible scene and an invisible scene. The Roman soldiers were seen by the disciples nailing Christ's physical body to the cross where He suffered and died. This was the visible scene. Behind this visible scene, there was an invisible scene. Man could not see this scene, but the angels could see it. In that invisible scene, Christ was stripping off the rebellious angels,

Read

the rulers and authorities in the air, coming to bother Him. When Christ was crucified on the cross, He was not only damaged by the physical soldiers of the Roman Empire, but in the invisible scene, the rulers and the authorities, the fallen angels from the air, came to trouble Him. Christ stripped them off, just as a person would strip off a jacket.

Even though Christ was in the likeness of the flesh of sin, He still had the flesh. The rulers and the authorities of the rebellious angels came to get that flesh, and they tried to remain on that flesh. Thus, He had to strip them off, indicating that this was a battle. This can be compared to a person trying to strip off a jacket while someone else is trying to keep this jacket on him. Christ, however, overcame these rebellious angels by stripping them off and making a display of them openly in the cross. This means that He shamed them openly. Man could not see this invisible scene, but all the angels, both good and bad, saw it. Christ triumphed over these rebellious angels in the cross.

Colossians 2:15 is a piece of the big puzzle of Christ's death, but who has collected this piece? We need to see that while Christ was being crucified on the cross, He was struggling with all the evil angelic rulers and authorities. Christ on the cross did not deal merely with sin and with Satan. Satan is not that simple. He has many followers. According to Revelation 12:4, one-third of the angels followed Satan in his rebellion. He had a big following, and among all these rebellious angels, some are the rulers and authorities in the air.

Satan has a kingdom in a realm that covers the air, the earth, and the water. In the air, Satan has angels; on the earth, Satan has the fallen people; and in the water, Satan has the demons (Eph. 2:1-2; Matt. 8:31-32; 12:43-44). Satan has a kingdom of which he is the ruler and the king. He has his subordinates in the air, his subjects on the earth, and his evil servants, the demons, in the water. This shows us again that behind the visible scene, there is an invisible scene. This is why the nightclubs and sinful places of amusement are so attractive to fallen man. Behind these things there is the unseen world of the fallen angels and demons.

read

3. Dealing with the Old Man

Christ's death also dealt with the old man. In ourselves we all are old because we belong to the old man. The old man is not the originally created man, but the fallen created man.

a. To Crucify Our Old Man

Romans 6:6a says that our old man has been crucified with Christ. This includes everything related to our old man, such as our thinking, our likes and dislikes, and our good temper and bad temper.

b. To Terminate the Old Creation,
Which Is Related to the World

Christ's death terminated the old creation, which is related to the world. Galatians 6:14 says that the world was crucified on the cross. Then verse 15 says, "For neither is circumcision anything nor uncircumcision, but a new creation is what matters." This shows that the crucifying of the world is related to the new creation. If we do not go through the cross, we cannot be a new creation. On one side of the cross is the old creation, and on the other side is the new creation. When we pass through the cross, the old creation becomes the new creation.

In our life-study of the book of Daniel, I pointed out that the crucifixion of Christ, the Messiah, the Anointed One (Dan. 9:26), is a landmark between the old creation and the new creation. The old creation was terminated on the cross at Christ's death, so Christ's death becomes a landmark between the old creation and the new creation. We were the old creation, yet we have all been brought to the cross. On the cross we were terminated, and this termination ushered us into Christ's resurrection in which we all have been germinated to become the new creation. The new creation needs the crossing out of the old creation.

c. To Kill the Natural Life
with Its Natural Ability

The cross dealt with the old man to kill the natural life with its natural ability (2 Cor. 4:10a, 11a, 12a, 16a). A person who is very capable may do many things by his natural ability, but that ability should be broken. The apostle Peter had his natural strength and ability, and he thought he was stronger than the other disciples. He told the Lord Jesus that even if all the others were stumbled, he would never be stumbled (Matt. 26:33). Then the Lord said, "Before a rooster crows, you will deny Me three times" (v. 34). The Lord allowed Peter to fail utterly in denying the Lord to His face three times (John 18:17, 25, 27), so that his natural strength and self-confidence could be dealt with. Then after the Lord's resurrection, He came back and asked Peter three times if he loved Him (21:15-17). The intention to love the Lord is right, but to love the Lord by our strength and by our ability is wrong. That is natural, and anything natural must be crucified.

Second Corinthians 4 shows us that to the apostle Paul the Lord's death became a constant killing. We may use today's medicine as an illustration of how we can experience this killing. In an antibiotic there is the killing element to kill the germs. Today the all-inclusive Spirit is our divine antibiotic. In the all-inclusive Spirit, there is the killing element of Christ's death. Paul said in 2 Corinthians 4 that he was under the killing of the death of Christ all the time. This death kills our flesh and our natural man. 2 Cor 4:10-12

In verse 16, Paul said that his outer man was decaying, being consumed, being wasted away, or being worn out. Our outer man is being consumed. Before a brother gets married, he may not be consumed that much. Many times the most consuming element to a brother is his wife and then his children. The wife is a big "cross," and the children are small "crosses" to him. To be crossed out is to be consumed. The parents need to be crossed out, consumed, by their children. The killing of Christ is a consuming.

Brother Watchman Nee referred to this consuming as the breaking of the outer man in his book entitled *The Release of the Spirit.* If the outer man is not broken, the inner spirit cannot be released. At the end of his ministry, Brother Nee always talked about the breaking of the outer man, which is the killing of the death of Christ.

d. To Crucify the Flesh with Its Passions and Its Lusts

Galatians 5:24 says that they who are of Christ Jesus "have crucified the flesh with its passions and its lusts." The flesh with its passions and its lusts has been crucified on the cross.

e. To Make the Body of Sin of No Effect

Through Christ's death on the cross, the body of sin was annulled, or made of no effect, that we should no longer serve sin as slaves (Rom. 6:6b). Brother Nee said that Christ's death made the body of sin jobless, unemployed. The job of the flesh is to sin. Now the crucifixion of Christ has made our body of sin jobless, of no effect, that we should no longer serve sin as slaves. The flesh has lost its job. This is all related to the death of Christ dealing with the old man.

4. Dealing with the Law of the Commandments

The death of Christ also dealt with the law of the commandments.

a. To Abolish Its Ordinances

Through His death, Christ abolished the ordinances that the two, Israel and the Gentiles, might be created into one new man in Christ, thus making peace (Eph. 2:15; Col. 2:14). The main ordinances among the Jews were the keeping of the Sabbath, circumcision, and the dietary regulations. The Jewish religion is built upon these three pillars. These became a strong factor of separation, separating the Jews from all the Gentiles.

Furthermore, all of the different cultures have their ordinances. The Japanese and the Chinese have their specific ordinances. The Texans have their ordinances, and the Yankees have their ordinances. But all of these ordinances have been crucified. The middle wall of partition, the wall of separation, has been torn down by Christ's death. Now regardless of our race or culture, we all can be one in Christ.

With all of the ordinances, we could have never been the one new man. How can the Chinese and the Japanese, and

Jew commandment : ① Sabbath day
⑤ circumcision
⑥ No pig , unt unclean foot animals.
THE ALL-INCLUSIVE DEATH OF CHRIST   73

the whites and the blacks be one new man? They can be one
new man because Christ slew all the ordinances and crucified
all the natural persons on the cross. Now in the new man,
there is room only for Christ. In the new man, Christ is all
and in all (Col. 3:11).

b. To Slay the Enmity between Israel and the Gentiles

Through His all-inclusive death, Christ slew the enmity
between Israel and the Gentiles that the two might be reconciled to God in one Body (Eph. 2:16). He created the two into one
new man and reconciled both in one Body. The one new man is
the one Body. As the Body of Christ, the church needs Christ as
its life, whereas as the new man, the church needs Christ
as its person. With the new man, the person is Christ, and
with the Body, the life is the Spirit. Both Christ and the Spirit
are one, and the new man and the Body are also one. All the
separations have been crucified on the cross, and we have
been reconciled to God in one Body.

B. On the Positive Side

Now we want to see two aspects on the positive side of
Christ's death.

1. To Release the Divine Life

Christ's all-inclusive death released the divine life from
the shell of His humanity (John 12:24). In incarnation Christ
put on humanity, and that humanity became a shell to con-
ceal the divine life. The divine life was hidden, concealed, in
Christ's humanity, and this humanity had to be broken on the
cross. Christ's death released the divine life from His human
shell. He was the one grain falling to the earth to die for the
release of His life.

2. To Impart the Released Divine Life
into the Believers

Through His death, Christ imparted the released divine
life into the believers, making them many grains for the constitution of the Body of Christ (John 12:24; Rom. 12:5; 1 Cor.
10:17). This is the positive side of Christ's death: to release

the divine life from Himself as the one grain and to impart the divine life into many grains so that the Body could be constituted for Christ's counterpart.

III. THE SYMBOLS OF THE TWO ASPECTS OF CHRIST'S ALL-INCLUSIVE DEATH

Now we need to see the symbols of the two aspects of Christ's all-inclusive death. These two symbols in John 19:34 are blood and water.

A. The Blood Symbolizing the Redeeming Death of Christ

The blood symbolizes the redeeming death of Christ. The blood is for redemption. In this sense Christ's death is a redeeming death.

B. The Water Symbolizing the Life-releasing and Life-imparting Death of Christ

The water symbolizes the life-releasing and life-imparting death of Christ. The purpose of this is to produce the Body of Christ.

We need to get into all the crucial points of this message to know the all-inclusive death of Christ. All the negative things in the whole universe have been cleared up by the death of Christ. Today if we are going to live the Christian life, we must live it through the death of Christ. "If no death, no life" (see *Hymns,* #631—chorus).

THE ALL-INCLUSIVE
RESURRECTION OF CHRIST

Scripture Reading: John 11:25; 10:17-18; Acts 10:41; 2:24; 3:15; Mark 2:8; Luke 23:46; Heb. 2:14; Col. 2:15; 1 Pet. 3:18b-19; Phil. 3:10a; Rom. 6:9; Eph. 2:6; 1 Cor. 15:45b; Acts 13:33; Rom. 8:29b; 1 Pet. 1:3; Rom. 8:9-11; Exo. 30:23-25; Eph. 3:8; Rom. 8:13b; 1 John 2:20, 27; Phil. 3:10

In order to stay healthy as human beings, we need to eat the proper food and take the proper medicine. Today there has been much scientific study concerning food and medicine to help people to be healthy and stay healthy. The Bible tells us that in our Christian life, the Word of God is food (Matt. 4:4; Jer. 15:16) and medicine to us (Prov. 4:20-22). In 1 Timothy, 2 Timothy, and Titus, Paul spoke of healthy teaching (1 Tim. 1:10; 2 Tim. 4:3; Titus 1:9; 2:1), healthy words (1 Tim. 6:3; 2 Tim. 1:13), and healthy speech (Titus 2:8). *Healthy* implies the matter of life. The healthy teaching with the healthy words and healthy speech ministers the Word as the supply of life to people, either nourishing them or healing them. Because the Word is our food and medicine, we need a scientific study of it to help us to be healthy and stay healthy in our Christian life. In particular, we need a scientific study of the all-inclusive Spirit, who has been compounded with the elements of Christ's all-inclusive death and all-inclusive resurrection.

We have seen that the all-inclusive Spirit is typified by the compound ointment in Exodus 30:23-25. This ointment is a compound of five elements. Olive oil is the basic element, signifying the unique God. This element is compounded with four other elements, which typify various aspects of the death and resurrection of Christ. Exodus is a book of types. If we do not understand the types, we cannot understand Exodus. Pharaoh was a type, Egypt was a type, and even all the calamities used by God to punish Pharaoh are types. We need to understand the truths in the Bible through its types.

One of the great types in the Bible is the type of the compound ointment in Exodus 30. We need a scientific study of such a wonderful type of the all-inclusive Spirit. Because of the scientific study of food and medicine, people are healthier and live longer today. Nearly every medicine in the United States today has been studied scientifically. Such a study of the all-inclusive Spirit with the elements of Christ's death and resurrection really helps us to be healthy in the Christian life. In this series of messages on the Christian life, we want to present all the things we have dug out of the Word in our scientific study.

Actually, organic things are altogether mysterious and beyond our natural understanding. Anything that is related to our physical life is mysterious, but studying the things of our physical life helps us to be healthy. It is the same with the plant life. If we study the plant life, we can do the things necessary to keep plants healthy. We want to have a scientific study of the things of the divine life so that we can be healthy in the Christian life. In this message we want to see the crucial things concerning the all-inclusive resurrection of Christ.

I. RESURRECTION CONQUERING DEATH

Life could be subdued by death, but resurrection conquers death; hence, resurrection is stronger than life. We have to investigate this statement. Was the Lord Jesus' life subdued? If you say "yes," I say "no"; and if you say "no," I say "yes." If His life was not subdued, how could He have been killed? In Acts 3:15, Peter told the men of Israel that they had killed the Author of life. The Lord Jesus' life could be subdued because He was killed. Eventually, however, He was not subdued. He was subdued temporarily for three days, but after three days He was not subdued. Apparently, visibly, and physically, He was subdued. But intrinsically, invisibly, and spiritually, He was not subdued.

When He was crucified on the cross, He was stripping away

all the rulers and authorities as spoken of in Colossians 2:15. Furthermore, when He was buried physically in the tomb, His spirit was very active. After dying in the flesh, Christ was still active in His spirit to proclaim to the spirits in prison, to the rebellious angels, God's victory through Him over Satan (1 Pet. 3:18b-19). While Christ's body was buried in the tomb, He was active in His spirit in Hades, so He was not subdued. Eventually, He conquered death, and death was subdued. He walked out of death. Thus, on the one hand, He was subdued by death; on the other hand, He was not subdued by death.

II. BEFORE HIS DEATH CHRIST BEING NOT ONLY LIFE BUT ALSO RESURRECTION

Before His death, Christ was not only life but also resurrection. Before His death He told Martha, "I am the resurrection and the life" (John 11:25). Christ was the resurrection before He died. This is beyond our understanding, but it is a divine fact.

III. CHRIST HAVING AUTHORITY TO LAY HIS LIFE DOWN OF HIMSELF AND HAVING AUTHORITY TO TAKE IT AGAIN

Christ had authority to lay His life down of Himself, and He had authority to take it again (John 10:17-18). The Greek word for life here is not the eternal life, but the soul-life, psuche. Visibly, Christ was arrested and put to death by others, but actually He laid down His soul, His human life, of Himself to accomplish redemption for us. After three days, He exercised His authority to take His life back in resurrection.

IV. IN THIS SENSE, CHRIST'S RESURRECTION BEING HIS RISING FROM THE DEAD BY HIMSELF

In the sense of His having authority to lay His life down and to take it again, Christ's resurrection was His rising from the dead by Himself (Acts 10:41). This is on the active side. Christ had the authority to take His life back, so He rose up. The Bible says that He rose from the dead (1 Thes. 4:14a). This means that He gained the victory.

V. BUT IN THE SENSE THAT HE WAS KILLED
BY LAWLESS MEN,
HIS RESURRECTION WAS
HIS BEING RAISED UP BY GOD

In the sense that Christ was killed by lawless men, His resurrection was His being raised up by God (Acts 2:24; 3:15). To rise up is active. To be raised up is passive. On the one hand, He rose up from the dead by Himself. But on the other hand, He was raised up by God.

VI. CHRIST GOING TO PROCLAIM
TO THE FALLEN ANGELS
THE VICTORY ACHIEVED BY GOD
THROUGH CHRIST'S DEATH ON THE CROSS

First Peter 3:18b-19 reveals that while His body was buried in the tomb, Christ in His spirit, which is His spiritual nature (Mark 2:8; Luke 23:46) and which was made alive, enlivened, with new power of life, was active and went to proclaim to the fallen angels the victory achieved by God through Christ's death on the cross (Heb. 2:14; Col. 2:15). While men were crucifying, killing, Jesus on the cross outwardly and visibly, God was also doing something to enliven Christ with new power of life. First Peter 3:18b says that on the one hand, He was put to death in the flesh, but on the other hand, He was made alive in the spirit. His spirit was made alive by God when He was being crucified on the cross, and in this empowered spirit, He made a proclamation to the fallen angels after His death in the flesh and before His resurrection. This was a precursor to His resurrection. Before He rose up from the dead, He was active in His spirit among the dead in Hades.

VII. BY HIS RESURRECTION POWER
CHRIST CONQUERING DEATH
AND COMING OUT OF DEATH
THAT HE MAY DIE NO MORE

By His resurrection power (Phil. 3:10a), Christ conquered death and came out of death that He may die no more (Rom. 6:9). From the day of His resurrection, Christ is no longer subject to death.

He only has both passive & active voice. We only have passive voice.

THE ALL-INCLUSIVE RESURRECTION OF CHRIST   79

VIII. THE BELIEVERS OF CHRIST BEING RAISED UP WITH CHRIST IN HIS RESURRECTION

The believers of Christ were raised up with Christ in His resurrection (Eph. 2:6). We have seen that Christ's resurrection has two aspects. First, He Himself rose up from the dead. The verb here is in the active voice. Second, He was raised up by God from the dead. The verb here is in the passive voice. But we do not have two aspects, two voices, to our resurrection. We did not rise up from the dead, in the active voice. Instead, we were raised up by God, in the passive voice.

IX. IN SUCH A RESURRECTION THREE MARVELOUS MATTERS TRANSPIRED

A. Christ as the Last Adam Being Made a Life-giving Spirit

In such a resurrection three marvelous matters transpired. The first matter is that Christ as the last Adam, that is, as the last man in the flesh, became a life-giving Spirit (1 Cor. 15:45b). This is a great truth in the Bible!

In 1977 we fought for the truth concerning the Triune God. We published a booklet entitled *What a Heresy—Two Divine Fathers, Two Life-giving Spirits, and Three Gods!* Some at that time were saying that there were two Fathers—the Father in the Gospels and the Father in Isaiah 9:6 who is called the Father of eternity. They said that the Father in Isaiah 9:6 is not the holy Father in the Trinity. Instead, according to them, to say "the Father of eternity" is similar to saying that Edison is the father of electricity. But there is not another Father in addition to the Father in the Godhead. It is heretical to say this. They also said that the life-giving Spirit in 1 Corinthians 15:45b does not refer to the Holy Spirit. But besides the Holy Spirit who gives life, is there another Spirit who gives life? Of course, there is not. The Holy Spirit is the Spirit who gives life (2 Cor. 3:6b), the life-giving Spirit.

We have spoken the truth concerning Christ being the Spirit in many messages. I am happy to hear the saints at the Lord's table praise the Lord for becoming the life-giving Spirit. This shows that we have received the spiritual education of this divine truth. In our hymnal, there are also a number of hymns which speak of Christ being the Spirit (*Hymns,* #490, 491, 493, 539). Thy & Thine difference ?

B. Christ in His Humanity
Being Begotten by God in His Resurrection
to Be the Firstborn Son of God

Christ in His humanity was begotten by God in His resurrection to be the firstborn Son of God (Acts 13:33; Rom. 8:29b). John 1:18 says that Christ is the only begotten Son, who is in the bosom of the Father. In His glory in eternity past, He was the only begotten Son of God. Since He was the Son of God, why did He need to be begotten of God? This was because God needed a firstborn Son.

Christ was the Son of God in eternity past, but He became flesh (John 1:14). His flesh was human, not divine. This human part was surely not related to the divine sonship. His human part had to be begotten of God. For this purpose, I invented a new word—"sonized." Christ's humanity had to be sonized in His resurrection. In His resurrection, He brought His humanity into divinity, making this humanity something divine. Christ in His humanity was sonized, begotten by God, in His resurrection.

C. All the Believers of Christ
Being Regenerated by God the Father
through the Resurrection of Christ

All the believers of Christ were regenerated by God the Father through the resurrection of Christ (1 Pet. 1:3). In His resurrection, we all were begotten by God to be His many sons. The firstborn Son of God and the many millions of sons of God were begotten at the same time in one "delivery." I once read of a woman who had seven children in one delivery, but the delivery of Christ's resurrection delivered a countless number of sons of God.

We need to remember that the resurrection of Christ produced three big matters: (1) the life-giving Spirit, (2) the firstborn Son of God, and (3) the many sons of God. The life-giving Spirit, the firstborn Son, and the many sons of God are altogether for the Body of Christ, which is the organism of the Divine Trinity. *Christ's* resurrection is not an event, but a person.

X. THE LIFE-GIVING SPIRIT AS THE RESURRECTED, PNEUMATIC CHRIST BEING THE REALITY OF CHRIST'S RESURRECTION

The life-giving Spirit as the resurrected, pneumatic Christ is the reality of Christ's resurrection (Rom. 8:9-11). In His resurrection, Christ became altogether pneumatic. When Christ was in the flesh, He was visible. But He became the life-giving Spirit in resurrection, and now He is invisible. The Lord Jesus is in us and in our midst in our gatherings, but He is invisible. He is pneumatic.

I learned what the word *pneumatic* means by seeing this word on the tire of a car. To be pneumatic is to be full of air. For us to be pneumatic as Christians is for us to be full of the Spirit, full of the divine air. Now in His resurrection the very Christ who was in the flesh is entirely pneumatic and invisible. Even though He is invisible and pneumatic today, He still has a spiritual body, a body of glory (1 Cor. 15:44; Phil. 3:21).

XI. THE RESURRECTION OF CHRIST BEING AN ELEMENT OF THE COMPOUNDED ALL-INCLUSIVE SPIRIT AS THE COMPOUND OINTMENT

The resurrection of Christ is an element of the compounded, all-inclusive Spirit as the compound ointment (Exo. 30:23-25); this makes the resurrection of Christ all-inclusive in the riches of Christ (Eph. 3:8). We call the life-giving Spirit the *all-inclusive Spirit* because He is now the compound Spirit. In Exodus 30:23-25 we see the compound ointment as a type of the compound Spirit. This ointment is composed of oil compounded with four spices: myrrh, cinnamon, calamus, and cassia. Myrrh signifies the death of Christ. Cinnamon signifies the sweetness and effectiveness of Christ's death. Calamus, a plant that shoots up into the air out of a marshy place, signifies the resurrection of Christ. Cassia was used in ancient times as a repellent to drive away snakes and insects. It signifies the repelling power of Christ's resurrection. Today the compound Spirit has been compounded with all of the elements of Christ's death and resurrection.

The numbers related to the compound ointment in Exodus are also full of significance. There is one unit of olive oil and four spices. These four spices are in three units of five hundred shekels each. *One* indicates the unique God, *three* refers to the Trinity, and *four* refers to the creature. In this Spirit is Christ who is God, the divine One, and man, the human one. This Spirit also has all the elements of Christ's all-inclusive death and all-inclusive resurrection. Thus, this Spirit is an all-inclusive dose. We cannot find God outside of these elements.

If we are going to enjoy God, we must enjoy this compound Spirit. Our God today has been consummated to be the compound Spirit. When I was a young Christian, I was told that God is in Christ. You cannot find God outside of Christ because God is in Christ. But what is Christ? Christ today is the all-inclusive Spirit (2 Cor. 3:17). In this all-inclusive Spirit, we have all that Christ is. We have the highest humanity, Christ's resurrected humanity. Christ's death and resurrection are also in this compound Spirit. The very Spirit working upon us and within us is such an all-inclusive, compound Spirit.

XII. THE COMPOUND SPIRIT BEING THE REALITY OF CHRIST'S RESURRECTION AND APPLYING THE RESURRECTION OF CHRIST TO CHRIST'S MEMBERS THROUGH THE DISPENSING OF THE DIVINE ANOINTING

The compound Spirit is the reality of Christ's resurrection and applies the resurrection of Christ to Christ's members through the dispensing of the divine anointing (Rom. 8:11, 13b; 1 John 2:20, 27). The all-inclusive, life-giving Spirit is the reality of the resurrection of Christ. If you have this Spirit, you are in the resurrection of Christ. If you do not have this Spirit, the resurrection of Christ has nothing to do with you.

XIII. THE BELIEVERS OF CHRIST KNOWING CHRIST THROUGH THE EXPERIENCE OF THE POWER OF HIS RESURRECTION

The believers of Christ should know Christ through the

experience of the power of His resurrection which conforms them to His death in the fellowship of His sufferings (Phil. 3:10).

All of the above organic items concerning the all-inclusive resurrection of Christ are mysterious and invisible, yet they are real. For example, our physical life is real, and it is working all the time, yet we are not aware of it. When we are healthy, our organic, physical life is active and working all day long, but we are not aware of its working. On the other hand, when we are sick, we are full of feeling that something is wrong. It is the same with the working of the organic, divine life within us. Christ is within us as the pneumatic One, as the compounded One, with God's divinity, Christ's humanity, and all the elements of Christ's person, of His death, and of His resurrection. Something organic is going on within us that we cannot fully understand, yet it is so real. This is altogether the moving, the acting, and the working of the pneumatic Christ who is the all-inclusive, life-giving, compound Spirit. We need to know Christ through the experience of the power of His all-inclusive resurrection, with which the all-inclusive Spirit has been compounded.

We cannot eat fish,

and asks us whether we've eaten the fish?

If we didn't eat, then where does the thing come from?

It's organic. We don't understand.

Teaching the word of God was the entertainment and amusement of bro. Lee

Food

He've either full of truth,

or full of lie.

Medicine.

All-inclusive spirit   All-inclusive resurrection

CHAPTER EIGHT

THE COMPOUNDING OF THE SPIRIT

Scripture Reading: Gen. 1:2b; Judg. 3:10a; Psa. 51:11; Isa. 63:10-11; Luke 1:15, 31-35; Matt. 1:18, 20; John 7:39; Rom. 8:2, 9; Acts 16:7b; Phil. 1:19b; 2 Cor. 3:17b, 18b; Exo. 30:23-30; 1 John 2:20, 27

In this message we want to see the compounding of the Spirit. I hope that this truth can be transfused into our being. The Christian life is altogether a matter of the Spirit. "No Spirit, no Christian life." John 4:24 says that God is Spirit. If we do not know the Spirit, we are through with God. As long as we are through with God, we are through with the Christian life. The revelation of the Spirit in the Bible is crucial. My burden is not to teach theology or biblical doctrines, but to minister the healthy teaching concerning the real Christian life. The real Christian life is altogether a matter of the Spirit.

In the first half of this century, there were two prominent and strong inner life teachers. They were Jessie Penn-Lewis and T. Austin-Sparks. I would say that they are the ones who ended the inner life movement.

The inner life movement began with Madame Guyon, Father Fenelon, and others in the seventeenth century. They are known as mystics, and their teaching as mysticism. Madame Guyon and Father Fenelon never left the Catholic Church, but they were very strong in the inner life. With them, however, the inner life was too mysterious and became a difficult thing for people to enter into and apprehend.

In the eighteenth century, William Law, a British scholar, improved the writings of the mystics, and this became a help to others. Later, Andrew Murray, a Dutch Reformed minister in South Africa, improved William Law's writing further. Andrew Murray was a speaker in the Keswick convention. His writing was very spiritual. His longest book is his exposition of the book of Hebrews entitled *The Holiest of All.* His masterpiece is a book entitled *The Spirit of Christ.*

After Andrew Murray, Jessie Penn-Lewis was raised up. She received help from Andrew Murray and became very prevailing. She stressed the subjective death of Christ. Her message was not on the objective cross but on the subjective cross. Some portions concerning the cross in Brother Watchman Nee's book *The Spiritual Man* mostly were translated from Mrs. Penn-Lewis's writings. Mrs. Penn-Lewis was also very strong in teaching concerning spiritual warfare. This teaching is in a book entitled *War on the Saints.* The section in *The Spiritual Man* concerning spiritual warfare is fully a translation from this book. Thus, Mrs. Penn-Lewis was very famous in two things: in the subjective death of Christ and in the spiritual warfare.

Following her, one of her co-workers by the name of T. Austin-Sparks was raised up by the Lord. He became prevailing in the teaching of the principles and life of Christ's resurrection. Thus, Sister Penn-Lewis, in the first quarter of this century, emphasized the death of Christ, and Brother Austin-Sparks, in the second quarter of this century, emphasized the resurrection of Christ. Both of them were strongly against Pentecostalism. If you read Brother Nee's *The Spiritual Man* carefully, you can realize that the writer of the section on spiritual warfare was a strong opposer of Pentecostalism. Mrs. Penn-Lewis considered Pentecostalism altogether as a demonic work. Brother Austin-Sparks was also absolutely against Pentecostalism.

They were both against Pentecostalism, but they also were very strong in the Spirit. Brother Austin-Sparks would not recognize any meeting as a church meeting unless that meeting was initiated by long prayer for the leading of the Spirit. He told me that every local church should be established by the leading of the Spirit through much prayer.

Because the Spirit is abstract and mysterious, many disregard and neglect the truth concerning the Spirit and the experience of the Spirit. The Southern Baptist denomination, the biggest and most fundamental denomination in the United States, discourages their preachers from speaking concerning the Spirit. They stress the Word, not the Spirit.

By this we can see that the bona fide, fundamental, real seekers of Christ all have problems related to the Spirit. The divisive factor among the fundamental, spiritual, and seeking Christians is not mainly related to doctrines. The divisive factor is nearly altogether due to the apprehension, comprehension, and realization of the Spirit.

There are different concepts concerning the Spirit because the Spirit is so mysterious and deep. God is a mystery, God's mystery is Christ (Col. 2:2), and Christ's mystery is the church (Eph. 3:4). The Spirit is also a great mystery. If this message concerning the compound Spirit could be understood, comprehended, and apprehended by us, the problems concerning the Spirit would spontaneously be solved. In order to receive the fellowship in this chapter properly, we not only need to exercise our spirit but also need to exercise our sober mind.

I. THE DIVINE TITLES OF THE SPIRIT IN THE OLD TESTAMENT

The first title of the Spirit in the Old Testament is *the Spirit of God*. This title is in Genesis 1:2. Genesis 1:1 says that in the beginning God created the heavens and the earth. Then verse 2 says that the Spirit of God brooded over the death waters.

The second divine title of the Spirit in the Old Testament is *the Spirit of Jehovah* (Judg. 3:10a). In Genesis 1 we have the title *God,* but in Genesis 2 we have another title, *Jehovah,* because in this chapter God begins to have contact with the man created by Him. Therefore, *Jehovah* is a title used for God's contact with man. It denotes God's relationship with man. Whenever God came to contact people in the Old Testament, He was the Spirit of Jehovah.

Psalm 51:11 and Isaiah 63:10-11 refer to *the Spirit of holiness,* but this is not a divine title of the Spirit. The King James Version translates *the Spirit of holiness* into *the Holy Spirit.*

This, however, is a wrong translation. "Thy Holy Spirit" in Psalm 51:11 should be "Your Spirit of holiness" according to the Hebrew, and "his Holy Spirit" in Isaiah 63:10-11 should be "His Spirit of holiness." *The Spirit of holiness* in Psalm 51:11 and Isaiah 63:10-11 is a description, not a title. It does not denote the third person of the Trinity. *The Spirit of holiness* refers to the nature and the essence of God. Andrew Murray pointed this out strongly. *The Spirit of holiness* is a description of what God is.

II. THE HOLY SPIRIT CONCERNS
THE INITIATION OF GOD'S NEW TESTAMENT ECONOMY
RELATED TO THE CONCEPTIONS OF
JOHN THE BAPTIST AND THE LORD JESUS

The title *the Holy Spirit* is not used in the Old Testament. It was used particularly at the time when the New Testament economy started—first at the coming of John the Baptist and then at the coming of the Lord Jesus. These two comings actually were one initiation of the New Testament economy. The New Testament economy was initiated by the conception of John the Baptist and the conception of the Lord Jesus. With these two conceptions, the Bible started to use a new divine title, that is, *the Holy Spirit*.

Actually, according to the Greek, the title *the Holy Spirit* can be translated literally as *the Spirit the Holy*. The Spirit of God, the Spirit of Jehovah, is *the Spirit the Holy*. *The Holy* refers to the separated One, the sanctified One. In the New Testament economy, everything must be separated unto God, sanctified unto God, made holy to God. The Spirit of God now is *the Spirit the Holy,* the Holy Spirit. The Holy Spirit concerns the initiation of God's New Testament economy related to the conceptions of John the Baptist and the Lord Jesus (Luke 1:15, 31-35; Matt. 1:18, 20). When the New Testament age began, the Bible used a particular name to denote the Spirit of God. The Spirit of God is *the Spirit the Holy,* the Holy Spirit.

The Holy The Spirit. ; The Spirit The Holy.

III. THE SPIRIT WAS NOT YET
BEFORE CHRIST'S RESURRECTION

John 7:39 reveals that the Spirit was not yet before

Christ's resurrection. The King James Version in John 7:39 says that the Spirit was not yet "given." The word *given* is in italics, meaning that it is not there in the original Greek text. The original Greek says, "The Spirit was not yet." The Spirit of God was there from the beginning (Gen. 1:1-2), but at the time the Lord Jesus spoke in John 7, the Spirit as the Spirit of Christ (Rom. 8:9), the Spirit of Jesus Christ (Phil. 1:19), was not yet, because the Lord had not yet been glorified.

According to John 7:39, the Spirit was not yet, "because Jesus had not yet been glorified." This indicates that the glorification of Jesus has everything to do with the Spirit's existence. According to Luke 24:26, Jesus was glorified when He was resurrected. Christ's resurrection, which was His glorification, was like the blooming of a flower. When a flower blooms, that is its resurrection and also its glorification. Christ's resurrection was Christ's "blooming," and that blooming was His glorification.

John 7:39 indicates clearly that before Christ's resurrection the Spirit was not yet. The Spirit of God was there, the Spirit of Jehovah was there, and even the Holy Spirit was there. From the conceptions of John the Baptist and Christ, the term *the Holy Spirit* began to be used. But when Christ came out to minister, the Bible tells us that before His resurrection, His glorification, "the Spirit was not yet."

The Spirit is the main subject in John 14—16. The Lord said that He would ask the Father to send the disciples another Comforter, who is the Spirit of reality (John 14:16-17; 15:26; 16:13). The Lord's speaking in John 14—16 was in the evening He was arrested. The next day He was crucified, and after three days He was resurrected. In resurrection He became a life-giving Spirit (1 Cor. 15:45b). In the evening of the day of His resurrection, He came back to the disciples, breathed into them, and said, "Receive the Holy Spirit" (John 20:22). At that time "the Spirit" as the Spirit of reality began to exist. This is clearly recorded in the New Testament, but in Christianity no one has paid attention to this except Andrew Murray.

Andrew Murray, in the fifth chapter of his book entitled *The Spirit of Christ,* speaks of the Spirit of the glorified

Jesus, the Spirit of the incarnated, crucified, and glorified Christ. In eternity past Christ was God; He was divine; He was altogether not human. The human element was not in Him in eternity past. He had only one unique element, that is, His divinity. But when He became incarnated, He picked up the flesh, that is, humanity. In His incarnation He became a God-man. This means He became One with two natures—the divine nature and the human nature. As God He has divinity; as man He has humanity. After His incarnation He is a person with two elements: the divine element, God, and the human element, man. Thus, He is the God-man with two natures, divine and human. He possesses both divinity and humanity.

While He was living on this earth, He was called Jesus. Before His resurrection, He was divine, but His humanity was not divine and spiritual. Jesus' body of flesh before His resurrection was not glorious, divine, spiritual, attractive, marvelous, splendorous, majestic, or excellent. Rather, according to Isaiah 53, Jesus was a person who was very lowly, with no attractiveness, no beauty, no comeliness (vv. 2-3; 52:14). But within His earthen vessel, within His humanity, there was God, who is divine. His divinity was concealed in His humanity. His divine Being was altogether contained in the earthen vessel of His humanity. Thus, His human part, in the thirty-three and a half years of His human living, was not divine, was not glorious.

In His human living, He lived in Nazareth in a carpenter's home for thirty years, and He ministered for three and a half years. He was a man who was altogether not glorious and even very lowly. Therefore, He was looked down upon and despised by many people. Some who despised Him said, "Is not this the carpenter...?" (Mark 6:3). He was not a glorious, divine carpenter. If He were, He would have become a great attraction. All the Jews would have streamed to Him in Nazareth. But when He came out, He had no outward beauty or comeliness for people to pay attention to Him.

His human shell concealed His divinity. This shell was altogether not handsome, beautiful, or comely. This means that He was a person with two natures, the divine nature and the human nature. The divine nature was glorious. Once, on a high mountain, He was transfigured for a short time (Matt. 17:1-2). Besides that short time, His divinity was concealed within His humanity for thirty-three and a half years. But on the mount of His transfiguration, the inner glory within Him swallowed up His outer humanity. Then He became glorious. That was a prefigure of His resurrection.

He was in a glorious divine nature and in a very low human nature for thirty-three and a half years. Then He died, and His death broke His human shell and released the inner, glorious, divine life (John 12:24). After three days, He entered into resurrection. When He became incarnated, He put on humanity. Then when He was resurrected, He brought His humanity into divinity.

Andrew Murray said that when Christ was resurrected, He sanctified His flesh. This means He made His humanity divine. He uplifted the human nature. Christ in His incarnation brought God into humanity, and in His resurrection He brought humanity into divinity. Andrew Murray used the word *interwoven* to describe this. By becoming incarnated and by being resurrected, Christ did an interweaving work. He interwove divinity into humanity and humanity into divinity. This is similar to the interweaving of two types of materials. Silk may be interwoven with cotton to produce a textile. We cannot say that this textile is only silk or only cotton. It is an interweaving of silk and cotton. In like manner, Christ is the interweaving of God and man. He was only God before His incarnation. But after His incarnation and through His resurrection, He became a God-man. God is now in humanity, and man is now in divinity. This is a kind of interweaving. Divinity was interwoven into humanity, and humanity was interwoven into divinity. Thus, divinity and humanity have become an interwoven cloth. Hallelujah, today we are wearing this cloth!

In reference to the resurrection of Christ, 1 Corinthians 15:45b says that the last Adam became a life-giving Spirit. This Spirit is the very essence, the very element, and the very reality of the resurrected Christ. The resurrected Christ today is the Spirit (2 Cor. 3:17). This is why we say that Christ is the pneumatic Christ. The pneumatic Christ is Christ as the pneuma, and the pneuma is the Spirit.

We have to realize that before Christ's resurrection there were the Spirit of God and the Spirit of Jehovah in the Old Testament and then the Holy Spirit in the Gospels. But after His resurrection, Acts 16:7b speaks of the Spirit of Jesus, and Romans 8:9 speaks of the Spirit of Christ. Then Philippians 1:19 speaks of the Spirit of Jesus Christ. The Spirit of Jesus Christ is "the Spirit" mentioned in John 7:39, the Spirit of the incarnated, crucified, and resurrected Jesus Christ.

IV. THE SPIRIT IS PARTICULARLY CALLED THE SPIRIT OF LIFE, THE SPIRIT OF CHRIST, THE SPIRIT OF JESUS, THE SPIRIT OF JESUS CHRIST, THE SPIRIT OF THE LORD, AND THE LORD SPIRIT

The Spirit of life (Rom. 8:2), the Spirit of Christ (Rom. 8:9), the Spirit of Jesus (Acts 16:7b), the Spirit of Jesus Christ (Phil. 1:19b), the Spirit of the Lord (2 Cor. 3:17b), and the Lord Spirit (2 Cor. 3:18b) are new terms for the Spirit in the New Testament. *The Lord Spirit* is a compound title like *the Father God* and *the Lord Christ*. The Spirit is the consummation of the Triune God. He is the consummated Triune God.

The Triune God was processed to become the all-inclusive Spirit. The first step of the Triune God's process was incarnation. The second step was human living, and the third step was His death. The fourth step was His resurrection. After going through such a "tunnel" of His process, He became a life-giving Spirit (1 Cor. 15:45b). The life-giving Spirit is the processed and consummated Triune God. This Spirit, the processed and consummated Spirit, is the consummation of the Triune God, who is both God and man, having both the divine nature and the human nature. Within Him there is the element of divinity. Within Him there is also the element of the sanctified and uplifted humanity.

V. THE SPIRIT IS A COMPOUND SPIRIT, TYPIFIED BY THE COMPOUND ANOINTING OINTMENT

The Spirit, after Christ's resurrection, is a compound Spirit, typified by the compound anointing ointment. Exodus

30:23-25 says, "Take thou also unto thee principal spices, of pure myrrh five hundred shekels, and of sweet cinnamon half so much, even two hundred and fifty shekels, and of sweet calamus two hundred and fifty shekels, and of cassia five hundred shekels, after the shekel of the sanctuary, and of oil olive a hin: and thou shalt make it an oil of holy ointment, an ointment compound after the art of the apothecary: it shall be a holy anointing oil." The compound anointing ointment in these verses is a unique type of the all-inclusive Spirit.

The Pentateuch, the first five books of the Old Testament, is full of types. The burnt offering, the meal offering, the peace offering, the sin offering, and the trespass offering are types (Lev. 1—7). The tabernacle is also a great type (Exo. 25:8-9; 40:1-2). In Exodus 30 there is also the wonderful, mysterious type of the compound ointment. We need to be impressed with the significance of this type.

The one hin of olive oil is the base of the compound ointment, and this oil is compounded with four spices—myrrh, cinnamon, calamus, and cassia. These five elements compounded together become an ointment. An ointment may be compared to paint. Paint is not merely oil, but it is oil compounded with other elements. The ointment in Exodus 30 is a compound of five elements. God told Moses to compound these five elements together to make an "ointment compound."

Before God's incarnation, there was only the divine element in the Spirit. But through His incarnation, human living, and death, this One became a life-giving Spirit in resurrection (1 Cor. 15:45b). His divinity, humanity, human living, all-inclusive death, and wonderful resurrection are compounded in the Spirit. When I was a young Christian among the Brethren, I heard them say that the compound ointment is a type of the Spirit, but they did not get into the details. It was not until 1954 that I received the light concerning the all-inclusive Spirit as signified by the compound ointment. I received much help from Andrew Murray's book *The Spirit of Christ*. Since 1954 the Lord has gradually shown us more and more concerning the details of the compound ointment.

The one hin of olive oil is a type of the unique God. Thus,

the compound Spirit is compounded with the divinity of God, typified by the one hin of olive oil. This is the base. Furthermore, the four spices are all of the plant life. In the Bible, plants signify humanity. Also, the number four signifies the creatures. In the ointment we have the one God with His creature, man. Thus, the compound Spirit is compounded with the humanity of Christ, typified by the four kinds of spices.

The Spirit is also compounded with Christ's death, typified by myrrh; with the sweetness and effectiveness of Christ's death, typified by cinnamon; with the resurrection of Christ, typified by calamus; and with the sweetness and power (especially in the sense of resisting and repelling) of Christ's resurrection, typified by cassia.

The all-inclusive Spirit has also been compounded in the Triune God, typified by the three units of five hundred shekels, with the second one being split. The second unit of five hundred shekels being split typifies Christ as the Second of the Divine Trinity who was split, crucified, on the cross. The unique Triune God, signified by the one hin of olive oil and the three units of five hundred shekels, has been compounded together with the created man signified by the four spices of the plant life.

The number five, with the five elements and the three units of five hundred shekels, signifies that the compound Spirit enables us to bear the responsibility of the divine things. The Ten Commandments are divided into two sets of five commandments on two tablets. The ten virgins in Matthew 25 are divided into five wise ones and five foolish ones. These sets of five indicate responsibility.

We human beings must bear responsibility every day. To do our duties, to work, and to walk we need ten fingers and ten toes. We walk by our ten toes, and we work by our ten fingers. Our ten toes and ten fingers are divided into fives. Our hand has one thumb with four fingers. The one thumb may be compared to the one hin of olive oil, and the four fingers may be compared to the four spices of the compound ointment. When God, pictured by our thumb, is added to us human beings, pictured by our four fingers, we are able to bear responsibility. With only four fingers and no thumb, we cannot pick up things to bear responsibility. In like manner, without God, man cannot do anything. Man needs God added to his being, just as the four fingers need the thumb added to them so that the hand can bear responsibility. The compound Spirit is the One that bears all the responsibility of the divine things.

VI. FOR THE ANOINTING OF THE THINGS RELATED TO THE WORSHIP AND SERVICE OF GOD AND HIS SERVING ONES, TYPIFIED BY THE TABERNACLE AND ITS UTENSILS AND THE SERVING PRIESTS

The compound ointment in Exodus 30 was used to anoint the tabernacle, all the utensils of the tabernacle, and the serving priests to make all these things holy, separated, sanctified, unto God for God's divine purpose (vv. 26-30). This indicates that everything related to the divine field must be anointed by the compound Spirit. The compound Spirit typified by the compound ointment is for the anointing of the things related to the worship and service of God and His serving ones (1 John 2:20, 27). When we are under the anointing of the Spirit, we can fulfill our duty to bear responsibility for the Lord's interest.

When we were saved, that was the beginning of our experience of the anointing by the compound Spirit. First, the Spirit came to inspire us to repent. He separated us from the common people so that we would come to Jesus. We were attracted by Jesus, we called on His name, and we believed into Him to be regenerated by the Spirit. After regeneration, we pass through the steps of sanctification, renewing, transformation, conformation, and eventually glorification. All of these are steps of the anointing.

First John 2:20 and 27 say that we have received the anointing of the Lord. Now we have to abide in the Lord according to this anointing. We have to walk, act, work, and have our being according to this anointing. This anointing is the working and the moving of the Spirit. Thus, Romans 8:4 says that we should walk according to the spirit. Then in Galatians 5 we are told to live and walk by the Spirit (vv. 16, 25). If we do not know this Spirit, how can we live the Christian life? It would be impossible.

Now we all have to ask where this compound Spirit is today. The New Testament reveals clearly and emphasizes very strongly that such a consummated Spirit is right in our spirit. Romans 8:16 says that the Spirit witnesses with our spirit that we are children of God. Second Timothy 4:22 reveals that the Lord as the Spirit is with our spirit. If we are going to live the Christian life, we must return to our spirit and remain there.

In our Christian life, we do not need to wait to hear a voice from the heavens. The experience of the compound Spirit is mysterious yet very normal. He is within us, but often we have no feeling that He is within us. However, whether we sense Him or not, He is in our spirit. Thus, we have to stay, to remain, in our spirit. Then we will walk, act, work, and speak according to the spirit. The spirit referred to in Romans 8 is actually a mingled spirit, the compound Spirit mingled with our human spirit.

It is by this compound Spirit that the death of Christ is applied to us. It is also by this Spirit that the resurrection of Christ is applied to us. The more we walk, live, move, act, and speak according to the spirit, the more we are in the Christian life. Some may say that Christ is life, but they cannot tell others how Christ can be life to them. The messages in this series on the Christian life show us how Christ as life can be applied to us.

All of us need to be clear about the significance of the compound ointment as a type of the compound Spirit. In order to have a clear revelation of the Spirit, we must be clear about this type. This is similar to our vision of the human government on earth. In order to see the situation of human government on earth from the divine viewpoint, we must be clear about the significance of the great human image in Daniel 2. If we do not understand the significances of that human image, we cannot understand human government in the biblical sense. In Exodus 30 there is a type of the compound Spirit. This is a particular, unique type. This type is beyond our human thought and realization, yet it must be interpreted.

As children of God, we are obliged to understand the type of the compound ointment. We must understand this type in order to understand the Spirit, just as we must understand that great human image in Daniel 2 in order to understand the prophecy concerning the political government on this earth in God's economy. The significance of the type of the compound ointment in Exodus 30 is greater than the creation of the universe. This type shows us that eventually our Triune God, after passing through all the processes, has become this ointment. Our processed and consummated Triune God is this ointment.

Day after day and moment after moment this ointment is working, moving, acting, and speaking within us. This moving of the ointment, this anointing, teaches us concerning all things. The anointing is the working, moving, acting, and speaking of the ointment, and the ointment is the consummation of our Triune God. We can see now that this type of the compound ointment in Exodus 30 is marvelous.

What is the Christian life? The Christian life is the acting, moving, working, and speaking of the consummated God who is typified by the compound ointment. In this life, both God and man are applied to us. We are a poor man, a low man, but we have an uplifted man, a man of the divine standard, in this anointing. In this anointing, we also have Christ's death and His death's effectiveness, which is so sweet. We have been forgiven, justified, and reconciled to God through His death so that we could be regenerated to be sons of God. How sweet is the effectiveness of His death as typified by the cinnamon!

Then in this anointing, we have Christ's resurrection applied to us. Christ's resurrection is so powerful, especially in the sense of resisting and repelling the enemy and all the negative things. This is typified by cassia, which was used in ancient times to repel insects and snakes. Christ's resurrection resists all the opposition and attacks from the enemy, and it repels all the evil "insects" and "snakes." Christ's resurrection is repelling all the demons, evil spirits, and especially their leading one, the snake, the old serpent, the devil.

The Christian life is not the living out of our natural human virtues. These good things, along with the evil things, belong to the tree of the knowledge of good and evil. Only the Christian life that is revealed in the Scriptures as the moving and working of the indwelling compound Spirit belongs to the tree of life. I hope that the fellowship in this message will give us a clear picture of the Christian life.

CHAPTER NINE

THE SPIRIT'S APPLICATION
OF CHRIST'S DEATH AND
ITS EFFECTIVENESS

Scripture Reading: Rom. 8:9-10; 2 Cor. 4:10a, 11a, 12a; Rom. 6:6; Gal. 2:20a; 5:24; Rom. 8:13b; Matt. 16:24; Rom. 8:6b; Gal. 5:16, 25; Rom. 8:4b; 1 Cor. 15:36; John 12:24; Rom. 8:13b; 2 Cor. 4:10-11

In this message we want to see the Spirit's application of Christ's death and its effectiveness. This is very mysterious, but it is definitely revealed in the Bible. Christ, the person, and His death and resurrection are one entity. This is logical, but it is not easy to understand. Why is it that Christ's resurrection and His death are one with Himself?

If we had only Christ without His death and resurrection, we would have a Christ without a way of application. Christ's riches, Christ's contents, are altogether wrapped up with His death and resurrection. We saw in the previous message that Christ, His death, and His resurrection are compounded together in the Spirit. This compounding makes Christ, His death, and His resurrection one entity.

THE REAL HISTORY OF THE UNIVERSE

In order to see the great importance of the compound Spirit and of its application, we need to see the major items in the history of the universe. In the universe, first there was God, the Triune God. Even in eternity past, God was triune. The Father, the Son, and the Spirit coexist eternally. The Bible shows us that the Father, the Son, and the Spirit are one God and that They are eternally coexistent.

The eternal Triune God created the universe, but the universe was altogether outside of God. God still remained by Himself in His divinity. God and the universe were fully separated. God was in the universe, but God stood alone, by Himself, leaving His universe also alone by itself.

Then God created man. Man was made in God's image and according to God's form (Gen. 1:26). After creating man, however, God still existed apart from the universe and from man. Even though man was bearing His image and form, God still existed by Himself. God and man were separate. Man lived apart from God, and man was not united with God.

About four thousand years after the creation of man, God became a man. He was conceived in the womb of a virgin. Conceiving is a mingling, a blending. About two thousand years ago, the unique God, who had been existing for a long time, came into man. That was the incarnation. Incarnation brought divinity into humanity. Through incarnation the Triune God was not only united with man but also blended with man. The issue of this blending is a man in the universe who is the mingling of God with man, and His name is Jesus. Jesus is the complete God and the perfect man. He is God and man mingled together. God, in Christ, is mingled with man.

The first item in the history of the universe is God; the second item is the created universe, and the third item is man. The fourth item is the mingling of the first and the third items. Jesus Christ is the mingling of God and man. The Bible in Isaiah 9:6 says that He is wonderful. This verse also says that a child is born to us and a son is given to us, yet His name is called the eternal Father. Isaiah 7:14 says that a virgin will conceive and bear a son, and she will call His name Immanuel. These verses show that the Son is the Father and that the Child is God. Immanuel means God with us. Jesus is God with us. He is God and He is also God incarnated to dwell among us.

This One is God—the Father, the Son, and the Spirit—and this One is also a man. This man is wonderful in what He is, wonderful in His Being. Jesus is a wonder in the universe because He is God the Father, God the Son, God the Spirit,

Suffering. It's the divine enjoyment that brings us through.
brings us into glory.
(Not to focus on)

and also a man. Is He not a wonder? He is the fourth major item in the history of the universe.

The fifth item is Christ's death. His death was a joint venture. God the Father, God the Son, God the Spirit, and man were all involved in the death of Christ. They all were joined in a joint venture to accomplish redemption. There is a group of stars in the universe in the form of a cross, which is called the Southern Cross. Jessie Penn-Lewis, in her speaking about the cross of Christ, referred to this group of stars. This shows that Christ's death is a great thing in the universe.

The sixth major item in the history of the universe is the resurrection of Christ. The principle of resurrection is involved with all kinds of living things. In the book of Isaiah, the kingly family of David was likened to a big tree. One day this big tree was cut down to the very root. Only a short stem was left. Isaiah 11:1 says, "Then a twig will come forth from the stem of Jesse, And a branch from his roots will bear fruit." Christ as a twig came out of the stem of Jesse. This twig eventually became a branch. Here we can see the principle of resurrection. Christ's coming was the resurrection of the kingly family of David. The principle of resurrection can also be seen in nature. When a seed is sown into the earth, it dies and then it rises up. This is resurrection. The New Testament tells us that Christ rose up from the dead.

The seventh major item in the history of the universe is that in and through His resurrection, Christ became a life-giving Spirit (1 Cor. 15:45b). We have seen in the previous message that the life-giving Spirit is a compound, as typified by the compound ointment in Exodus 30:23-25. The life-giving Spirit has been compounded with God as the base, typified by the one hin of olive oil, and with man, typified by the four spices. This all-inclusive Spirit is also compounded with all the elements of the process through which God has passed. In this compound there is the death of Christ, signified by myrrh, and the resurrection of Christ, signified by calamus. There is also the effectiveness of the death of Christ, signified by cinnamon, and the repelling power of the resurrection of Christ, signified by cassia.

egg - whole remain perfect, useless. Broken. death. resurrection on small hem.

No Spirit, no God, no Father, no Spirit.

No Spirit, no death of Christ, no resurrection No Spirit, no sanctification no repelling no glorification

[Stop. say Hallelujah!]

to head up all things = uplift Christ
Exalt Christ.

102   THE CHRISTIAN LIFE
live by the Spirit. Walk by the Spirit

The one hin of oil and the three units of five hundred shekels among the spices signify the unique Triune God. The second unit is split into two, signifying that the Second of the Divine Trinity was split on the cross. In the compound Spirit we have God, the Father, the Son, the Spirit, and the uplifted Man. In the compound Spirit, we also have Christ's death, the effectiveness of Christ's death, Christ's resurrection, and the repelling power of Christ's resurrection. The compound Spirit is the totality of all of these items. God, God the Father, God the Son, God the Spirit, the uplifted Man, the death of Christ, the effectiveness of His death, the resurrection of Christ, and the power of His resurrection are compounded together, blended together, to be the compound life-giving Spirit.

Today where is God? We have to say, "In the Spirit." Where is the Father? "In the Spirit." Where is the Son? "In the Spirit." Where is the Spirit? "In the Spirit." Where is the uplifted Man? "In the Spirit." Where is the death of Christ? "In the Spirit." Where is the effectiveness of the death of Christ? "In the Spirit." Where is the resurrection of Christ? "In the Spirit." Where is the power of the resurrection of Christ? "In the Spirit." Thus, if we have the Spirit, we have everything.

When we have some sensation that God is with us, we are sensing the Spirit. When the husbands are about to argue with their wives, they may experience something within urging them to stop. At that juncture, they are sensing that the Spirit is there with the death of Christ. Without the Spirit, we cannot experience the death of Christ, because His death is in the Spirit.

We need to realize that without the Spirit, we cannot experience anything of God in His economy. No Spirit, no God the Father. No Spirit, no God the Son. No Spirit, no God the Spirit. No Spirit, no uplifted, glorified Man. No Spirit, no death of Christ. No Spirit, no effectiveness of the death of Christ. Without the Spirit, the death of Christ is far away from us in time and space. But with the Spirit, Christ's death is here to kill us, to crucify our old man. No Spirit, no resurrection. No Spirit, no salvation. No Spirit, no regeneration.

X Sinless Perfection.
It's not about being perfect.
Exalt you. (us).   V-S. Exalt Christ

No Spirit, no renewing. No Spirit, no sanctification. No Spirit, no transformation. No Spirit, no conformation. No Spirit, no glorification. Every positive thing in this universe in the economy of God is compounded in this Spirit. Today we can see, by God's enlightenment, the all-inclusiveness of the Spirit.

The Spirit is the totality of God, of the Triune God, of the uplifted Man, of the death of Christ, of the effectiveness of this death, of the resurrection of Christ, and of the power of this resurrection. This is why the New Testament charges us to live by the Spirit, to walk by the Spirit (Gal. 5:16, 25), and to do everything according to the spirit (Rom. 8:4). The only way to exalt Christ, express Christ, manifest Christ, and live Christ is to live, to walk, and to do things according to the spirit. If we love others in ourselves, we exalt ourselves. But if Christ loves others in us and through us, He is exalted.

John Wesley thought that holiness was sinless perfection, but according to the principle of the Bible, even if we could arrive at sinless perfection, that would not exalt Christ but ourselves. That would not express Christ but ourselves. To live by the Spirit, walk by the Spirit, and do things according to the spirit is to live Christ, to magnify Christ, to manifest Christ, to express Christ, to exalt Christ, and to glorify Christ.

In the compound Spirit, we experience the killing of Christ's death. When we live and walk by the Spirit, the Spirit becomes a killing to our soul, our natural man, and our body with its practices. The Spirit is an all-inclusive dose which both nourishes us and kills the negative things in our being. Even the physical food that we eat nourishes us and helps to kill the germs in our being. Today the pneumatic Christ, the all-inclusive Spirit, is our life, light, food, drink, and air so that we can be spiritually nourished and so that the negative things within us can be killed. We have to eat, drink, and breathe in the pneumatic Christ, who today is the life-giving, compound Spirit. I would consider the life-giving Spirit as the seventh major item in the history of the universe.

The eighth item is the church, and the ninth item is the New Jerusalem. The issue of our enjoyment of the compound Spirit first is the church and consummately will be the New Jerusalem. These nine items are the real history of the universe.

CHRIST'S DEATH AND ITS EFFECTIVENESS, WITH WHICH THE SPIRIT HAS BEEN COMPOUNDED, BECOME PREVAILING IN THE SPIRIT

Now we want to see the Spirit's application of Christ's death and its effectiveness. Christ's death and its effectiveness, with which the Spirit has been compounded, become prevailing in the Spirit. If Christ's death were not in the Spirit, His death could not be prevailing. If we enjoy and experience the Spirit, His death becomes prevailing in us. The death of Christ is in the Spirit.

THE COMPOUNDED SPIRIT DWELLING IN OUR SPIRIT TO DISPENSE CHRIST'S DEATH AND ITS EFFECTIVENESS FROM OUR SPIRIT TO OUR SOUL AND EVEN TO OUR MORTAL BODY

The compounded Spirit dwells in our spirit to dispense Christ's death and its effectiveness from our spirit to our soul and even to our mortal body (Rom. 8:6, 9-10). This dispensing is the anointing (1 John 2:20, 27), and the anointing is the moving of the indwelling Spirit. Those Christians who love the Lord and maintain fellowship with the Lord, always have the feeling and sensation that something is moving within them. That moving is the anointing, and that anointing is the dispensing of the Triune God, of the death of Christ, and of the resurrection of Christ. That dispensing comprises all these elements: divinity, Christ's humanity, Christ's death, the effectiveness of His death, Christ's resurrection, and the power of His resurrection.

When we are under this dispensing, our natural life is killed, and our flesh is crucified. It is under this dispensing, this anointing, this moving of the indwelling Spirit, that we experience the death of Christ. When we are about to lose our temper, we may stop ourselves and go to pray. After our prayer, our anger is over. This is because our prayer activates the moving of the indwelling Spirit, and within this moving there is the killing power.

THE PUTTING TO DEATH OF JESUS IN OUR ENVIRONMENT COOPERATING WITH THE INDWELLING SPIRIT TO KILL OUR NATURAL MAN

The putting to death of Jesus in our environment cooperates with the indwelling Spirit to kill our natural man (our outer man), comprising our body and our soul. This is mentioned emphatically in 2 Corinthians 4:10-12. Paul said that he was bearing about in his body the putting to death of Jesus that the life of Jesus might be manifested in his body.

We have the indwelling Spirit within us, but because we are sometimes stiff-necked and stubborn, God raises up the environment to deal with us. The entire situation of our living rises up against us to help the indwelling Spirit. The indwelling Spirit works to kill us. The Spirit is the Killer, but He needs an instrument, a "knife," to kill us. The "knife" may be a brother's wife, his children, or certain brothers and sisters in the church. A certain saint can become a "knife" which the Spirit uses to kill us.

We all like to have a nice environment, with everything smooth, peaceful, sweet, and nice. When people ask us, "How are you?" We always say, "Fine." Many times when we say this, however, we are lying. If we were fully honest, we would respond by saying, "Not so good." This is because we are under an environment of sufferings and pressures which works with the Spirit to kill our natural man. Brother Nee referred to this kind of environment as the discipline of the Holy Spirit. The putting to death, the killing, in 2 Corinthians 4 is through the environment. In speaking about the application of Christ's death, Romans 8 refers to the indwelling Spirit, while 2 Corinthians 4 refers to the outward environment. The outward environment cooperates with the inward Spirit to carry out the killing of our natural man.

Second Corinthians 4:16 says, "Our outer man is decaying, yet our inner man is being renewed day by day." The word *decaying* means "being consumed, being wasted away, being worn out." According to the Chinese translation of the Bible, it can also mean "being destroyed." As our outer man is being consumed by the killing work of death, our inner man is being renewed with the fresh supply of the resurrection life.

COOPERATING WITH THE OPERATING SPIRIT
AND ACCEPTING THE ENVIRONMENT
IN OUR SPIRIT, SOUL, AND BODY

We should cooperate with the operating Spirit and accept the environment in our spirit, soul, and body. In every part of our being, we must be willing to cooperate with the indwelling Spirit and to accept the outward environment. Then we are acting under the killing of Christ. This killing is carried out by the indwelling Spirit with the environment as the killing weapon.

In order to cooperate with the operating Spirit and accept the outward environment, we need to recognize that we have been crucified with Christ (Rom. 6:6; Gal. 2:20a). We also need to crucify our flesh with its passions and its lusts (Gal. 5:24). In one sense, we cannot crucify ourselves. But in another sense, we can crucify our flesh with its passions and lusts because we have the new man. The new man crucifies the flesh. This is why we need to exercise our spirit, the new man, to crucify our flesh, our outer man.

We also need to put to death, by the Spirit, the practices of our body (Rom. 8:13b). To put to death means to kill. We need to kill the practices of our body. Whatever our body of sin does, needs to be killed. To gossip on the telephone is a practice of the body which needs to be killed.

We need to bear the cross, that is, to remain in the crucifixion of Christ (Matt. 16:24). We should not depart from the crucifixion. We have to stay in the crucifixion, to bear the cross. We also need to stay in our spirit and to live by and walk according to the spirit—the mingled spirit (Rom. 8:6b; Gal. 5:16, 25; Rom. 8:4b).

Such an experience of the death of Christ brings in His resurrection—if there is no death, there is no life. In 1 Corinthians 15:36 Paul said, "What you sow is not made alive unless it dies." The Lord's word in John 12:24 reveals this principle. The grain of wheat needs to die. Otherwise, it cannot be multiplied. Romans 8:13 also implies this principle. This verse says that if by the Spirit we put to death the practices of our body, we will live. This is the resurrection brought in by our experience of Christ's death. Second Corinthians 4:10-11 shows that the killing of the cross results in the manifestation of the resurrection life. This daily killing is for the release of the divine life in resurrection.

We should not forget that if there is no death, there is no life. The death of Christ is in the compound Spirit. The Spirit is the application of the death of Christ and its effectiveness. What is the Christian life? The Christian life is a life which is all the time under the killing by the compound Spirit. If there is no killing, there is no life. In everything we do, we need to be killed. In our shopping, in the way that we cut our hair, and in our home we need to be killed in our natural man.

In the church life, we cannot avoid being killed. Every saint in the church is a "knife" to kill our outer man. The longer we stay in the church, the more we experience the killing, the working of death, the working of the cross. We need to remain under the killing, the working of death, the working of the cross, that we may live in resurrection. This is glorious. Even this is our happiness, our joy. We need to experience the Lord's killing, His putting to death, every day. Then we will daily have the victory and joy in Christ's resurrection.

CHAPTER TEN

THE SPIRIT'S APPLICATION
OF CHRIST'S RESURRECTION
AND ITS POWER

Scripture Reading: 1 John 5:6; Rom. 8:11, 6b, 10; 2 Cor. 4:16, 11; Col. 2:12; Eph. 2:6a; Phil. 3:10; 2 Cor. 4:10, 16; 12:9; 13:14; 1 Cor. 15:10, 45b, 58

In this message we have come to one of the most mysterious matters in the Bible—the resurrection of Christ. First, God Himself is resurrection. This was why the Lord Jesus, when He was about to resurrect the dead Lazarus, told Martha that He is the resurrection (John 11:25). He is not only life but also resurrection. In the entire universe, apart from God, apart from Christ, there is no resurrection. God is resurrection. God is a mystery, and this mystery is resurrection. Then this mystery eventually became the consummated Spirit.

WHAT RESURRECTION IS

For many years I did not have much understanding of what resurrection is. I received much teaching concerning Christ's death, but I did not have a full realization of Christ's resurrection. But today I can tell you that resurrection is a threefold mystery. God, resurrection, and the Spirit are the constituents of this threefold mystery. Resurrection originates with God and is consummated in the all-inclusive, life-giving, compound Spirit.

The consummated Spirit is the reality of the resurrection of Christ. The resurrection of Christ can be realized and experienced only in the Spirit. Without the Spirit, we cannot know the resurrection. Resurrection is a person. Resurrection is God. God passed through the processes of incarnation, human living, crucifixion, and resurrection to become the life-giving Spirit (1 Cor. 15:45b). The Spirit is the consummation of God as the resurrection.

Today if the Spirit were taken away from us, we would no longer be Christians (Rom. 8:9b). Furthermore, if the Spirit were taken away from the Bible, the Bible would become a book just of dead letters. It would become merely a storybook with no reality. The reality of the Bible is the Spirit as the consummation of resurrection, and resurrection is the embodiment of the processed God.

In our Christian experience, we experience the Spirit daily, but due to the lack of adequate teaching among today's Christians, we do not realize that our experience of the Spirit is our experience of the resurrection of Christ. Today there are a number of people who talk about how to be filled with the Spirit. But if we do not realize that the Spirit is the resurrection, we cannot have the adequate experience of the Spirit. As long as we experience resurrection, that is the real experience of the Spirit, both essentially and economically.

Christ breathed the Spirit into the disciples (John 20:22), and He poured out the Spirit upon the disciples fifty days later (Acts 2:1-4). This was after His resurrection. Before His resurrection, there was no possibility of having the essential Spirit entering into our being, and no possibility of having the economical Spirit poured out upon us. Both of these matters took place based upon the fact that resurrection was consummated. It was the resurrection of Christ that made the Spirit available and applicable. His entering into us as the essential Spirit is for life, and His being poured out upon us as the economical Spirit is for power; these two aspects of the Spirit are the parts of the reality of the resurrection of Christ.

Acts is a book of the testimony of the resurrection of Christ. Acts mentions clearly that the disciples were witnesses (1:8), witnessing of the resurrection of Christ. Today, Christians preaching the gospel stress the death of Christ. But the early apostles, like Peter and Paul, stressed the resurrection of Christ in their preaching of the gospel. Of course, they also spoke of the death of Christ, but this death is not the consummation. The consummation is resurrection.

Resurrection is the Spirit, and the Spirit is the processed and consummated Triune God. God, Christ, and Christ's death and resurrection have been compounded into this one compound Spirit, who is the very reality of Christ's resurrection.

Resurrection is a person because Christ said that He is the resurrection. Life and light are also a person. Christ said that He is the life (John 14:6) and the light (John 8:12). Love is also a person. The Bible says that God is love (1 John 4:8, 16). But no verse says that Christ is death. We can say *Christ's* death, using the possessive case, because death is not the consummation. The consummation is resurrection. The processes through which the Triune God passed consummated in resurrection. Thus, resurrection is the very consummated God.

We must have a clear view of the resurrection. God is the resurrection, the resurrection is the compound Spirit, and the compound Spirit is the consummated God. This view of the resurrection is according to the divine revelation of the Holy Bible.

EXPERIENCING RESURRECTION

The Christian life is a life in Christ's resurrection. To know the Spirit, we have to know resurrection. Resurrection is the Triune God consummated to be the life-giving Spirit. We are not able to understand such a deep and high mystery, the mystery of resurrection, but we can experience resurrection. We do not even understand our human life, but we can experience this life daily. When we eat food, we take in many nourishing elements and vitamins which we do not understand, yet we can enjoy them. We do not know what human life is, but we can surely enjoy this life.

Who can fully understand the Triune God? We cannot understand the Triune God, but He is available for us to experience and enjoy. Nearly every morning, my first prayer is somewhat like this: "Thank You, Lord, for the peace. Thank You for the safety. Thank You for Your presence. Thank You for Your cleansing. Thank You for Your forgiveness. Thank

You for Your preserving of my health." This is a simple prayer, but through this simple prayer, I enjoy the Triune God and I am filled with the Spirit. I have been enjoying the Triune God for close to seventy years. I cannot deny there is a God, because day by day I enjoy Him as resurrection.

The God whom we contact is resurrection. When we contact God, resurrection functions in us, and everything is under our feet. When resurrection functions in us, we are full of joy, full of peace, full of rest, full of praising, and full of rejoicing. When we are experiencing the Spirit as resurrection, all the negative things are on the cross, in the tomb, and under our feet.

Human life is full of troubles, worries, and all kinds of sorrows. We can rid our being of these things only by our God who is resurrection, which is the Spirit. The Spirit kills, and the Spirit also resurrects. This is because Christ's killing death and His uplifting resurrection are compounded in the compound Spirit, whom we are enjoying. As we enjoy the compound Spirit, we are experiencing the inner killing and the inner resurrecting. As long as we have this killing plus the resurrecting, we have God. Killing plus resurrecting is God. God moves in us, works in us, functions in us. He gives us Himself as patience, peace, and power to endure sufferings. He gives us Himself as everything we need to live the Christian life.

God is mysterious, resurrection is mysterious, and the compound Spirit is also mysterious. The Bible has much to say about these three items, but they are mysterious to the uttermost. Even though they are so mysterious, they are real in our daily experience in the Christian life.

We need to experience the Spirit's application of Christ's resurrection and its power all the time. The full-time trainees need to enter into this experience in their limited environment. Five sisters may live in one apartment unit. In this apartment, each of them has to do everything carefully. Otherwise, they can offend one another. This apartment is like a small "tomb" to them. To be in the full-time training is a suffering, but in this suffering, there is joy and peace. If we try to escape from the environment which God has arranged for us, we will not have joy and peace. When we stay in this limited environment, we can experience resurrection.

In order to experience resurrection, we also need to be limited in our speaking. The more we gossip, the more resurrection is gone. The more we gossip, the more there is no Spirit in our experience. To experience the Spirit as the reality of resurrection, we need to turn to our spirit to pray, praise, sing, or talk to God. The title of Psalm 18 indicates that this psalm was David's conversation with God, his talk to God. We need to talk to God and consult with Him. After ten minutes of talking to God, we will be on fire and full of the Spirit as the reality of resurrection.

THE SPIRIT BEING THE REALITY
OF CHRIST'S RESURRECTION AND ITS POWER

The Spirit is the reality of Christ's resurrection and its power, with which the Spirit has been compounded (1 John 5:6).

THE SPIRIT, COMPOUNDED WITH
CHRIST'S RESURRECTION AND ITS POWER,
INDWELLING OUR SPIRIT

The Spirit compounded with Christ's resurrection and its power indwells our spirit (Rom. 8:11) to dispense Christ's resurrection and its power not only to our spirit and soul (Rom. 8:6b, 10; 2 Cor. 4:16), but also to our mortal body (Rom. 8:11; 2 Cor. 4:11).

COOPERATING WITH THE RESURRECTING SPIRIT

We should cooperate with the resurrecting Spirit to recognize that we have been resurrected with Christ (Col. 2:12; Eph. 2:6a) and to pursue the power of the resurrection of Christ (Phil. 3:10a). Paul said that he wanted to know Christ and the power of His resurrection. This power will conform us to Christ's death (Phil. 3:10b; 2 Cor. 4:10, 16).

The more we die, the more Spirit we have. The more we die, the more we are in resurrection. The more we die, the more the divine attributes, such as peace, joy, light, life, and love, will be with us to be the content of our human virtues.

This is the Christian life, and this is the great mystery of godliness (1 Tim. 3:16). Godliness is the living out of the Triune God, the very manifestation of the divine Being in our flesh.

We need to be people who are occupied with the Triune God, with the consummated Spirit, and with the resurrection. We need to be "crazy" Christians who are filled with the Spirit inwardly and outwardly. We should be fully in resurrection. What is resurrection? Resurrection is the processed, consummated Triune God as the compound Spirit.

CHRIST'S RESURRECTION WITH ITS POWER IN THE LIFE-GIVING SPIRIT BEING THE SUFFICIENT GRACE OF THE PROCESSED AND CONSUMMATED TRIUNE GOD

Christ's resurrection with its power in the life-giving Spirit is the sufficient grace of the processed and consummated Triune God (2 Cor. 12:9; 13:14; 1 Cor. 15:10, 45b, 58). We may also say that the Spirit as the realization of Christ's resurrection and its power is the sufficient grace. The sufficient grace is the compound Spirit as the reality of resurrection.

First Corinthians 15 proves this. This is a long chapter of fifty-eight verses on Christ's resurrection. In this chapter, Paul presents a rebuttal to those who say there is no resurrection (vv. 12-19). In verse 10a Paul also said, "But by the grace of God I am what I am." Grace here is the resurrected Christ as the life-giving Spirit. Paul went on to say, "I labored more abundantly than all of them, yet not I but the grace of God which is with me" (v. 10b). Paul labored more abundantly than all of the apostles by the grace which operated in him. The grace of God with him was the consummated Spirit, the consummation of the Triune God.

In verse 58 Paul said, "Therefore, my beloved brothers, be steadfast, immovable, always abounding in the work of the Lord, knowing that your labor is not in vain in the Lord." We should not be dismayed or disappointed. Instead, we should labor. We need to labor not by our self, not by our power, not by our strength, and not by our capacity, but by the compound, all-inclusive Spirit who is the reality of the divine resurrection, which is the Triune God Himself. Then our labor will never be in vain. This is the walk and the work of the Christian life. Actually, our work is our walking, our living.

Some people wonder when I will retire. I will retire only when I go to be with the Lord. This is because I have something within me making me "crazy." The Triune God, the resurrection, and the compound Spirit are my enjoyment. This is the experience of the grace of Christ, the love of God, and the fellowship of the Spirit being with us (2 Cor. 13:14). The consummated God, the resurrection, and the all-inclusive, consummated Spirit are our portion in the divine fellowship.

CHAPTER ELEVEN

LIVING AND WALKING BY THE SPIRIT

Scripture Reading: Gal. 5:25; 2:20a; Phil. 1:19-21a; Gal. 5:16a; Rom. 6:4; 8:4; Gal. 6:16; Phil. 3:16

In this message we will consider the matter of living and walking by the Spirit. This matter is crucial to the believers and crucial to the Christian life. Our living and walking by the Spirit include three main things—the all-inclusive Spirit, the all-inclusive death of Christ, and the life-releasing and producing resurrection of Christ. Apparently, according to the letter, these three things have nothing to do with one another. Actually, however, these three things are compounded into one. The Spirit in the New Testament is the compound Spirit, even the compounded Spirit. The compound ointment in Exodus 30 is the best type of the compound Spirit. That ointment was not made of only a single ingredient—olive oil—but was made of olive oil compounded with four kinds of spices.

We cannot see the Spirit, because He is invisible. We also have something within us that is invisible to us—our spirit. These two spirits—the Spirit and our spirit—are both invisible, yet they are more than real. According to our experience, we do have a part within us that the Bible calls our spirit (Job 32:8; Prov. 20:27; Zech. 12:1; Rom. 8:16; 1 Cor. 16:18; 1 Thes. 5:23; 2 Tim. 4:22). Moreover, God is Spirit (John 4:24). Although we cannot understand this, because we have a spirit, we can realize it by our own experience.

The Triune God has gone through all the processes in Christ to become the all-inclusive, compound Spirit. Today this Spirit is marvelous. In Him we have the Triune God, and in Him we also have the uplifted humanity. Without the Bible we cannot understand that in the Spirit, who is the divine

Spirit, there is the uplifted humanity, the humanity of the
highest standard. Furthermore, in the Spirit there is also
Christ's humanity with His human living. All these items
are in this Spirit. Even more, in the Spirit there is Christ's
death. Because this death is not simple, we have called it the
all-inclusive death. This death solved the problems and terminated the negative things in the universe, and this death also
released the divine life. We need to realize that in the Spirit
we have such a wonderful death. Finally, in this Spirit we also
have the life-releasing and producing resurrection of Christ.

LIVING AND WALKING BY THE MINGLED SPIRIT

"But I say, Walk by the Spirit and you shall by no means fulfill the lust of the flesh"

Galatians 5:16 and 25 speak of both living by the Spirit
and walking by the Spirit. Verse 25 says, "If we live by the
Spirit, let us also walk by the Spirit." According to this verse,
to live is one thing, and to walk is another. It is difficult for
Bible translators to decide which spirit is referred to in this
verse—the divine Spirit or the human spirit. In the Recovery
Version of the New Testament, we made a decision on this
verse according to the context. One way to read Galatians
5:25 in its context is to interpret the spirit in this verse as the
divine Spirit. However, it is also possible to interpret and
apply this verse in another way. The matter of living has
two aspects. First, to live means to have life, to receive life.
Second, to live is to have a living. To receive life is one thing,
and to have a living is another thing. Romans 1:17 and
Galatians 3:11, which are quoted from Habakkuk 2:4, say
that the righteous "shall have life and live by faith." According to these verses, we first have life, and then we live. To
have life is surely by the divine Spirit, but to live, that is,
to have a living, implies our human spirit.

The two spirits are implied also in the matter of walking
by the spirit. To walk surely is by the divine Spirit with
our human spirit. These two spirits—the divine Spirit and
the human spirit—are mingled within us; hence, we call this
spirit "the mingled spirit." Romans 8:4 says that the righteous requirement of the law is fulfilled "in us, who do not
walk according to the flesh but according to the spirit." Here
it is difficult to decide whether our walk should be according

to the divine Spirit or according to the human spirit. Actually, it should be according to both of these spirits, that is, according to the mingled spirit.

The Christian life is not simple. When I was a young Christian, I thought that the Christian life is simply a life of being good. However, we should not think that if we are humble, gentle, kind, and tolerant, we are holy and are living the Christian life. The Christian life is to live by the Spirit and then to walk by the Spirit. To walk means to have our being and implies everything in our daily human life. If we are quiet, we should be quiet by the Spirit. If we are quiet by our self, we are not living and walking by the Spirit. To be quiet is not wrong, but we should be quiet by the Spirit. A cemetery is a very quiet place, and none who are buried there make any noise. If we are quiet by the Spirit, we will not be like a dead person buried in a tomb; on the contrary, we will be very active and very living.

To live the Christian life, we must make many subtractions. We must subtract our natural life, our self, our goodness, and many other things. We must subtract everything until we have nothing further to subtract. Then, what is left will be the Spirit. As long as we still have something to subtract, we are still not living by the Spirit.

When we say "Hello" to others, we must do so by the Spirit. When we touch such details of our living, we can see that we are all very natural. After saying "Hello" to someone, we often say "How are you?" out of habit, without any consciousness or intention. We do not say such things by our spirit. However, to walk, to have our being, implies everything in our daily living. This means that we should be a person absolutely living by the Spirit and walking by the Spirit. The apostle Paul was one who practiced this. In 1 Timothy 4:7 Paul charged Timothy to exercise himself unto godliness. Godliness is the manifestation of God (1 Tim. 3:16). Thus, we need to exercise ourselves unto the manifestation of God. When we say "Hello," we need to ask, "Is this the manifestation of God?" If the answer is negative, we should not say that. Some may feel that this is too much. However, we do need to exercise ourselves to such an extent unto godliness.

When we are asked, "How are you?" most of the time we respond, "Fine." Such a response may not be by the Spirit. If we exercise ourselves unto godliness, we must hesitate when we answer such a question. In our hesitation, we need to consider how to answer in such a way that we exercise ourselves unto godliness, unto the manifestation of God. We must exercise ourselves to such an extent that all day long, whatever we are, whatever we do, whatever we think, whatever we express, and whatever we say must be the expression, the manifestation, of God. This surely must be done by the Spirit.

Thank the Lord that today both the divine Spirit and the human spirit are very definitely located. As believers in Christ, we all have a spirit, and our spirit has been regenerated by the divine Spirit. By this the two spirits have been located—in us. This is a wonder. Both of the two spirits are in us! Hence, wherever we are, these two spirits are with us. They have been located within us.

We, the believers, live the Christian life by exercising our spirit. We should learn to practice one thing: in doing anything, we should not do it hastily. When we are going to answer someone, we should not answer quickly; instead, we should consider whether or not we are answering in our spirit by the divine Spirit. In everything, we need to consider carefully. Of course, this is very difficult, but still we need to learn. I was born a Chinese, and the Chinese language is my mother tongue. When I began to study English, I found that mastering English pronunciation was very difficult for me. This has required much learning over many years. In a similar sense, we were born human, and we were reborn divine. Now, we the human beings must learn to live a human life by the divine life. This requires much learning because we do not know how to live by the divine life.

In learning to live a human life by the divine life, prayer is a great help. By nature I am a quick person. It is difficult for me to be slow and considerate. However, after much prayer I become a very slow and considerate person. Praying slows us down. This means that praying makes us more spiritual. Prayer causes us to live a human life by the divine life. If you come to ask me something and I have not prayed in half a day, I will probably answer you quickly. However, if you come to me immediately after my morning prayer, I will be very spiritual; I will not answer you quickly. Prayer slows us down because to pray is to exercise our spirit, and that spontaneously puts aside our emotion, our will, and our mind. Whenever we stir up our spirit by praying, we become a very careful person.

I have no interest in merely teaching the Bible. My burden is to help the saints to understand what Paul wrote in Galatians 5:16 and 25 concerning living and walking by the Spirit. It is very rare to meet a person who lives by the Spirit and walks by the Spirit. We should not take verses like Galatians 5:16 and 25 for granted. On the contrary, we must endeavor to understand what it means to live and walk by the Spirit.

LIVING BY THE SPIRIT

The matter of living by the Spirit is mentioned in Galatians 5:25. To live by the Spirit equals to have Christ living in us. Although we all are persons, we should not live by our self as the person; we must live by another person. The Christian life is a life in which we live by another person. As long as we live by our self as our person, that is not the Christian life. As Christians, we should not have only one person; we must have two persons. One person is our self, and the other is Christ. This Christ who is our person within us is pneumatic; He is the Spirit (2 Cor. 3:17).

The Spirit by whom we must live is Christ. As the life-giving Spirit (1 Cor. 15:45b), Christ is pneumatic. He is not only our life (Col. 3:4) but also our person (2 Cor. 2:10). To speak of living by Christ as our life may be somewhat abstract, but to speak of living by Christ as our person is more definite. A person is very definite, whereas life is somewhat abstract. Whether we live by Christ as our life or not is difficult to know, but whether we live by Christ as our person or not is very clear. To speak of living by our self or living by Christ means that there are two persons by whom we can live. We should not live by our self; we should live by another person—Christ. *we have another person living in us →Christ Unbelievers do not understand.*

Equaling to Have Christ
Living in Us, That Is, to Live Christ,
the Pneumatic Christ in Resurrection,
That Christ May Be Magnified in Us

To live by the Spirit equals to have Christ living in us (Gal. 2:20a), that is, to live Christ, the pneumatic Christ in resurrection, that Christ may be magnified in us (Phil. 1:19-21a). For Christ to be our person within us, He surely must be pneumatic, and He must be in resurrection. Before His incarnation He was God as the Spirit already, but the Spirit in the stage before incarnation was not the life-giving Spirit. The life-giving Spirit, who is the reality of Christ, is the Spirit after Christ's resurrection. In His resurrection Christ as the last Adam became the life-giving Spirit (1 Cor. 15:45b). Today this life-giving Spirit is the pneumatic Christ, the resurrected Christ.

We live Christ that Christ may be magnified in us. To magnify Christ and to live Christ are not two different things; rather, they are one. To live Christ is to magnify Christ, and the magnification of Christ is the real manifestation of God. Without the magnification of Christ, it would be impossible to have the manifestation of God. When we live Christ, surely we magnify Christ.

Our living by our self can be likened to copper. In comparison, our living of Christ can be likened to gold. The best copper may look very much like gold. In the living of some saints it may be difficult to discern whether they themselves are expressed or whether God is manifested. Copper and gold look somewhat alike, but they are different in essence. Because of their quiet and careful natural makeup, some of the saints may resemble Christ in their living. Actually, however, their living may not be the living of Christ but the living of themselves. In contrast, it is easier to discern whether a person who is very active and makes many mistakes is living Christ or living himself.

Taking the Spirit—the Realization
of the Resurrected Christ—as Our Person

To live by the Spirit is to take the Spirit—the realization

of the resurrected Christ—as our person (Gal. 2:20a). To live by the Spirit equals to have Christ living in us and equals taking the Spirit as our person.

WALKING BY THE SPIRIT

The Two Aspects of the Christian Walk

To live may mean to have life, but to walk means to have our being. The Greek words translated "walk" in Galatians 5:16 and 25 are two different words. They signify the two aspects of the Christian walk.

The General Walk in Our Daily Life, Implying a Common, Habitual Daily Walk

The first word, used in Galatians 5:16a, denotes the general walk in our daily life, implying a common, habitual daily walk. This walk is referred to also in Romans 6:4; 8:4; and Philippians 3:17-18. The walk in all these verses is the general walk in our daily life.

The Walk according to Rules, Referring to a Walk That Takes God's Unique Goal as the Direction and Purpose of the Christian Life

The second word for *walk*, used in Galatians 5:25, refers to a walk according to rules, that is, the walk in line, in an orderly, regulated manner (Gal. 6:16; Acts 21:24; Rom. 4:12; Phil. 3:16), referring to a walk that takes God's unique goal as the direction and purpose of the Christian life, by living in the new creation (Gal. 6:15-16), by pursuing Christ (Phil. 3:12, 16), and by practicing the church life (Rom. 12:1-5; Eph. 4:1-16), so that God's economy for the church may be fulfilled.

The first kind of walk is the daily walk for our daily living, and the second is a walk according to rules for the church. The church is our goal, and the church is also our purpose. We walk this way and we take this way as a rule because our human life has a goal and a purpose, and this goal and this purpose are to have the church life. The Christian life has two aspects. One aspect is the Christian daily life, the normal, habitual, common living in our daily life, with no particular goal or purpose in view. But we Christians should not be simply for our daily life. We Christians must be persons for the church. The church is God's goal, and the church is God's purpose. Because of this, we must have rules to regulate our walk. The three main rules for the second kind of walk are to live in the new creation, to pursue Christ, and to practice the church life, so that God's economy for the church may be fulfilled.

The majority of Christians today do not have the church life. Those who do not have the church life may stay home in the evening to watch television. However, we who practice the church life have a rule, and that rule is to attend the church meetings. To us, to attend the church meetings is a rule. Another rule is found in Philippians 3, that is, to pursue Christ. In verses 12 and 16 Paul made the pursuing of Christ a rule. This rule is for the church life. If we do not live Christ and pursue Christ, it will be difficult for us to have the church life. We are strict in pursuing Christ so that we may gain Him to live the church life.

Every human being has two aspects to his living—his common, daily life and his business life. A person who operates a business or has a job must go to the office every morning by a certain specified time. Thus, he must keep the rule, the regulation, of rising early every morning. Furthermore, he must go to the office five days a week. Then, on Saturday morning he is free to remain in bed for a longer time. On Saturday he still lives his life, but he does not live it for his job. Rather, he lives a common, daily life. Thus, every person must live two kinds of lives, one for his ordinary daily life and another for his job, for his purpose, his goal.

We Christians also should have two kinds of walks. The first is the general walk in our daily Christian life. Things such as overcoming our temper are included in this kind of walk. The second is a walk according to rules, a walk in line, in an orderly, regulated manner. This kind of walk includes things such as attending the church meetings and speaking in the meetings for the church life. In our Christian life people may realize that, because we are a Christian, we would not lose our temper. This is the testimony of our general, daily walk. People may know us also as those who attend the church meetings on the Lord's Day morning and on other nights of the week. This is the testimony of our walk according to rules.

In Galatians 6:15-16 Paul said, "For neither is circumcision anything nor uncircumcision, but a new creation is what matters. And as many as walk by this rule, peace be upon them and mercy, even upon the Israel of God." To live a new creation by walking according to the rule of the new creation is the second kind of walk, the walk by rules. We have been regenerated to be a new creation (2 Cor. 5:17); hence, we must walk by the rule, by the regulation, of a new creation. Because we are a new creation, and because we have a goal, a purpose, there are certain things that we would not do. The new creation is just the church life, the Body of Christ.

To have a goal, a purpose, requires us to live a life by rules. However, the second aspect of the Christian walk must be supported by the first. If we do not live the first kind of walk, we cannot have the second. If we are a loose person, a busybody who gossips all the time, we will not be able to live a life that is for the church. Our walk for a purpose, for a goal, must be supported by our general, daily walk.

To Walk in Christ's Resurrection, through His Crucifixion, and by the Compound Spirit

To walk by the Spirit is to walk in Christ's resurrection, through His crucifixion, and by the compound Spirit (Phil. 3:10; 1:19b). Christ's resurrection, Christ's crucifixion, and the compound Spirit are one entity. It is impossible to separate these three. This simply means that the compound Spirit in us is the reality of Christ as the embodiment of the Triune God. Thus, in brief, this compound Spirit is the consummation of the Triune God. In a more simple way, the compound Spirit is just the processed and consummated Triune God. This Spirit can never work in anything without the crucifixion of Christ. Hence, this Spirit always puts us to death (2 Cor. 4:10-12). If we desire to have the first kind of walk, we need to be crucified. Likewise, if we would have the second kind of walk, we need to be crossed out, to be crucified. Crucifixion always ushers us into resurrection, and that resurrection is the Spirit. These three things—the Spirit, Christ's crucifixion, and Christ's resurrection—are always together. To walk by being crucified, to walk in resurrection, and to walk by the Spirit are the same thing. Our walk by the Spirit is a walk by being crucified and a walk in resurrection. These three are one.

Whether we are walking by the Spirit or not is determined by whether we are crucified or not. We know whether we are walking by the Spirit by knowing whether we are crossed out or not. If you are not crossed out, even if you feel that you are full of the Spirit, you should not do or say anything. Without crucifixion there is no filling of the Spirit. Therefore, we must immediately take the cross to receive Christ's crucifixion. When we take Christ's crucifixion, instantly we are in resurrection, and the reality of resurrection is the Spirit.

I can testify that I am learning this kind of lesson every day. Very rarely do I answer people's letters immediately after receiving them. When we receive letters, we should ask, "Who will answer—me or the Lord?"

If we have the assurance that we are crossed out, immediately we are in resurrection, and the reality of that resurrection is the life-giving Spirit. Then, whatever we do, we walk by the Spirit through Christ's crucifixion and in Christ's resurrection. This is the Christian life.

CHAPTER TWELVE

LIVING AND WALKING
UNDER THE CRUCIFIXION OF CHRIST

(1)

Scripture Reading: John 3:5; Gal. 2:20a; 1 Cor. 15:36; Matt. 16:24-26; Gal. 5:24; Rom. 6:6; 8:13b; 2 Cor. 4:10, 16; Phil. 3:10

In the previous message, we saw that we need to be those who live and walk by the Spirit. In this message we want to see our need to live and walk under the crucifixion of Christ. To live and walk by the Spirit is to walk in Christ's resurrection, through His crucifixion, and by the compound Spirit (Phil. 3:10; 1:19b).

The crucifixion of the Lord on the cross has two significant aspects—the objective aspect and the subjective aspect. The objective aspect of Christ's death refers to His redemption. He died for our sins to redeem us. In other words, Christ died a vicarious death for us. This was the objective aspect He accomplished on the cross apart from us about two thousand years ago in the distant land of Palestine. There is also the subjective aspect of the death of Christ. Christ died on the cross not only for us but also with us (Gal. 2:20a). When He died on the cross, He was not dying by Himself. He died with us.

People have different opinions about who actually died on the cross. Some unbelieving Jewish scholars would say that a martyr by the name of Jesus died on the cross for his religious teachings. They would say that he was martyred on the cross by the Jewish religionists through the hands of the Roman government. Other unbelievers would say that Jesus was a great man with the highest ethics of human life. According to their opinion, such a great, good, and wise man, whose teachings were on the highest plane of human ethics, was killed by his opposers.

Among the believers of Christ, there are also a number of views concerning who died on the cross. Many believers of Christ are shallow and superficial, and in their spiritual understanding they are just at the threshold of God's economy. They know only that Christ died for them on the cross as their Savior. To them Christ was not merely a martyr or a good man but a Savior. This understanding is right, but it is only partially right. This is a shallow, superficial understanding of who died on the cross.

First Corinthians 15:3 says that the first thing Paul delivered to the saints in the gospel was that Christ died for our sins. The word *for* means that He died a vicarious death. We needed Him to die for us as our Substitute. As our Savior, He represented us to die for our sins to accomplish redemption for us. This is right, but this is not a deep understanding of the death of Christ. If we are to be those who live and walk under the crucifixion of Christ, we need a deeper understanding of Christ's death.

OUR IDENTIFICATION, UNION, AND
MINGLING WITH CHRIST

Recently, I looked at two books which I purchased in San Francisco twenty-nine years ago in 1963. One is called *Bone of His Bone,* and the other is called *Born Crucified. Bone of His Bone* is a reference to Adam's word when God presented Eve to him (Gen. 2:23). Adam was looking for a counterpart, and God presented to him all the animals one by one. Of course, all of these animals could not match him. Adam named every living creature, but not one matched him. Then God put Adam to sleep, opened up his side, and took out a rib. Genesis 2:22 says that with this rib God built a woman for Adam. The King James Version says that God "made" a woman, but this is an inadequate translation. The Hebrew text says that God "built" a woman. The rib of Adam was the building material with which God built a female. Then Adam woke up, and God brought Eve to Adam. When Adam saw

Eve, Adam said, "This is now bone of my bones, and flesh of my flesh." In typology the bone with which Eve was built signifies the resurrection life of Christ. "Bone of my bones" indicates that we, the members of the church as the Body of Christ, are parts of the resurrected Christ.

On the jacket of the book *Bone of His Bone,* the publisher says that Christ's death on the cross was not just for redemption but for identification. Identification here means union. Christ died so that we could be united with Him. He died on the cross not only for objective redemption but also for subjective union, subjective identification. The book *Bone of His Bone* says that the Christian life is not an imitation of Christ but a participation of Christ. To imitate Christ is wrong. Christ died on the cross and we cannot imitate that, but we can participate in Christ's death. We cannot imitate Christ, but we participate in Him and in all that He has accomplished.

This union between us and Christ began from incarnation. Before incarnation God was merely God, and man was man. God and man did have some kind of relationship and some transactions with each other before the incarnation, but there was no union between them. The thought of union is in the divine revelation. First Corinthians 6:17 says, "He who is joined to the Lord is one spirit." Some call this union a union of life. We have a life union with the Lord Jesus. We are identified with Him. However, even the word *identification* is not fully adequate, because it does not convey the full thought of the divine economy. An identification card may have our picture on it, but that picture is not the real, living person. This shows that our terminology in human language is always inadequate.

We need to see the revelation of the union of God and man, beginning from the incarnation. Incarnation is God in His second person, embodying the entire Divine Trinity, becoming a man. In other words, incarnation was the Triune God embodied in Christ becoming a man. This is God uniting Himself with man. John 1 says that the Word, who was God, became flesh (vv. 1, 14). Thus, the identification between divinity and humanity, or the life union between divinity and humanity, began with divinity being joined to the flesh. Thus, when God became a man, the union between God and man started.

When the Lord Jesus was crucified on the cross, He was crucified in His flesh. The flesh, to which the Triune God was joined, implies a lot. This flesh implies all of us. All of us are flesh. Therefore, the New Testament says that no flesh can be justified by the works of the law (Rom. 3:20; Gal. 2:16). *No flesh* here means no man, no person. As long as we are a descendant of Adam, we are flesh. The entire human race is flesh.

We need to consider the use of the word *flesh* in the Bible. After God created Adam, He put Adam to sleep, took a rib out of his side, and built that rib into a woman. When Adam awoke, he saw Eve and declared, "She is flesh of my flesh." Adam was saying that she was flesh and that he also was flesh. She was not something separate from Adam. Thus, both the male and the female are flesh. At that time, the flesh did not have any sin; it was pure and clean. But by the time of Genesis 6, the Lord said that man's sin had become very great and that man had become flesh (vv. 5-7, 12). In Genesis 6, *flesh* is not used in a positive sense but in a negative sense. From Genesis 6 the word *flesh* throughout the Bible mostly refers to the negative sense.

In 1 Corinthians Paul used the words *fleshy* and *fleshly* (3:1, 3). Fleshy is worse than fleshly. The Corinthians became not only fleshly but also fleshy. Fleshy denotes being made of flesh; fleshly denotes being influenced by the nature of the flesh and partaking of the character of the flesh. The apostle considered the Corinthian believers to be totally of the flesh, to be made of the flesh, and to be just the flesh. We may not be fleshy, but much of the time we are fleshly. This is because we live, act, and walk not according to our spirit but according to our flesh.

John 1:14 tells us that the Lord Jesus became flesh. Paul in Romans 8:3 said that God sent His Son in the likeness of the flesh of sin. By the time of Genesis 6, man had become flesh, something utterly sinful. Man became the flesh of sin. Christ became flesh, yet He was only in the likeness of the flesh of sin. Sin was not within Him (2 Cor. 5:21). In His flesh, in His humanity, there was no sin. He was only in the likeness of the flesh of sin. We thank the Lord for this revelation in Romans 8:3.

When Christ as the divine person became incarnated, He joined Himself in His divinity with us, the flesh. When He became flesh, He started His union with man. He identified God with man. This means that He brought God into union with man. He brought God into humanity. Incarnation brought divinity into humanity.

Now we need to consider when humanity was brought into divinity. Union requires two parties, so there must be a two-way traffic of divinity being brought into humanity and of humanity being brought into divinity. God united Himself with us; then He caused us to be united with Him. God's uniting Himself with us in His incarnation is a one-way traffic. Then in His resurrection, He brought us, the flesh, into divinity. This is the completion of a traffic of two ways.

The identification, the union, between God and man took a long time to accomplish. God made man about six thousand years ago. In Genesis 3:15 God promised fallen man that He would come as the seed of the woman, indicating His incarnation, but He did not come right away. After two thousand years, He repeated nearly the same promise to Abraham. He told Abraham that in his seed (singular) all the nations would be blessed (Gen. 22:18; Gal. 3:16). The seed of the woman in Genesis 3:15 would be the seed of Abraham, a descendant of Abraham. God waited for still another two thousand years to fulfill this promise. From Adam to Abraham, there were two thousand years; and from Abraham to Christ, there were another two thousand years. There were altogether four thousand years from the creation of Adam to the incarnation of Christ as the seed of the woman and the seed of Abraham.

God came to join Himself to the flesh, to us, to humanity. He lived on the earth in humanity for thirty-three and a half years. The "divine factory" did not produce the mingling of God and man in a quick way. For God to fully accomplish His union with man, He had to pass through human living, pass through death, and enter into resurrection. He did this to bring humanity, to which He had united Himself, into divinity.

The New Testament tells us that when He died on the cross, He died with us (Gal. 2:20a), because He died on the cross in the flesh, and we are the flesh. He was in union with us. The Lord Jesus was crucified in His flesh (1 Pet. 3:18; Col. 1:22). Christ's divinity was not crucified; divinity cannot be crucified. His divinity includes the eternal life, the resurrection life; nothing can kill it. Christ died in His flesh. In His flesh, in the condition of His flesh, He was killed. The flesh not only includes us but also refers to us. Christ died in the flesh, and this flesh refers to the entire human race. This means that He died on the cross with us.

In the book *Born Crucified* there are a number of good expressions. The author said that Christ not only died for us but also died with us. He died for us to redeem us, and He died and resurrected with us (Eph. 2:6) to identify us with Him. When He became incarnated, He identified God with man. When He died and resurrected with us, He identified us with God. This is a two-way traffic.

Now we need to ask where Christ is today. We have to answer strongly, "Christ is in us!" Christ has been located. Before Christ became a man, He was merely the universal, omnipresent God. But when He became a man, He became located. Before His incarnation, He was like a bird soaring everywhere in the air, but through His incarnation, He entered into a cage. He became located. Jesus was caged, limited. When He was in Jerusalem, He could not be in Galilee at the same time. He was caged in His humanity.

Before we were saved, we were soaring, wandering everywhere. I can testify that I was once wandering everywhere. But one day when I was nineteen years old, I believed in the Lord Jesus. At that time, I was caged. The cage into which Christ entered was the flesh, the human race. The cage into which we believers have entered is a wonderful cage. This cage is Christ! Today we are in Christ.

Positionally, we are in Christ, but at times in our experience we get out of Christ. Sometimes the enemy comes to open the door of the cage. Then we are released. When we get mad, we are out of the cage. Christ was caged when He united Himself with man. We were caged when we were united with God. In Christian theology, this is known as identification, but in our teaching, we do not usually use the term *identification*. Instead, we use the terms *union* and *mingling*.

Mingling is deeper than union. In the incarnation, God not only united Himself with man but also mingled Himself with man. If I clasp my hands together, my hands are in union with each other, but mingling is much more than this. When one item is grafted to another, the result is mingling. Sometimes in surgery, skin is taken from one part of a person's body and grafted to another part. Eventually, the two pieces of skin are not only united but also mingled together. When a branch from one tree is grafted to another tree, they are mingled together. In the same way, God was mingled with man in incarnation. Then in Christ's resurrection, man was mingled with God. This is why the New Testament tells us that we were crucified with Christ (Gal. 2:20a) and were resurrected with Christ (Eph. 2:6). Through Christ's death and resurrection we were not only united to Christ, to God, but also mingled with Him.

In our recent life-study of the book of Jeremiah, I pointed out that in God's new covenant (Jer. 31:33-34), we have been made God in His nature and in His life, but not in His Godhead. This is because we have been begotten of God (John 1:13). Dogs beget dogs; lions beget lions; and man begets man. Since your father is a man, and you are born of him, are you not a man? As believers in Christ, we have been born of God; we have been regenerated by God. God is our Father, and we are His sons. Since our Father is God, what are we, the sons? The sons must be the same as their Father in life and in nature. We have been born of God to be the children of God (1 John 3:1). Eventually, when Christ comes, He will make us fully the same as God in life and in nature (v. 2). However, none of us are or can be God in His Godhead as an object of worship. In a family, only the father has the fatherhood. The children of the father do not have his fatherhood. There is only one father with many children. The father is human, and the children also are human, but there is only one father. In the same way, God is our unique Father; only He has the divine fatherhood. But we as His children are the same as He is in life and in nature.

The early church fathers used the term *deification* to describe the believers' participation in the divine life and nature of God, but not in the Godhead. We human beings need to be deified, to be made like God in life and in nature, but it is a great heresy to say that we are made like God in His Godhead. We are God not in His Godhead, but in His life, nature, element, essence, and image.

REGENERATED CRUCIFIED AND DYING TO LIVE

When we were regenerated, we were crucified. The writer of the book *Born Crucified* quotes a French preacher who said that the church was "born crucified." Then he goes on to say that to be born here means to be regenerated. No one was born crucified in a physical sense, but every believer is regenerated crucified. This corresponds with the Lord's word in John 3:5: "Unless one is born of water and the Spirit, he cannot enter into the kingdom of God." It would be helpful to read note 5[2] on this verse in the Recovery Version. "Water" here refers to the water in John the Baptist's ministry. John said, "I baptize you in water unto repentance, but He who is coming after me...will baptize you in the Holy Spirit..." (Matt. 3:11). In this word of John the Baptist to the Pharisees, water and the Spirit are referred to definitely. Later, the Lord Jesus came to talk to Nicodemus, who was also a Pharisee. Surely he had heard John's word. Thus, the Lord told him that he had to be born of water and of the Spirit. The water refers to John's ministry, and the Spirit refers to the Lord's ministry.

To be born of water, according to John's ministry, is for the termination of people of the old creation. When we are buried in the water of John's ministry, this indicates that we realize that we are good for nothing but death. When people came to John to repent, John threw them into the water to bury them, to end them, to terminate them. When a sinner repents to God, he should repent to such an extent that he realizes he is good for nothing but death. Thus, he hands himself over like a corpse to the baptizer.

When we preach the gospel and lead people to repent and believe into Christ, we may tell them, "You have to realize that as a person who has repented and believed into Christ, you, as a person of the old creation, are now a dead person. You have handed yourself over to me as a corpse, and I will now put you into a tomb of water to terminate you." Paul tells us clearly in Romans 6:4 and Colossians 2:12 that in baptism we are buried together with Christ into His death. When we raise up a baptized one from the water, that indicates resurrection. In resurrection, we are now in the Spirit. Through the terminating water of death and the germinating Spirit, we are born spiritually. To be reborn through termination and germination is to be regenerated. Thus, every regenerated person is regenerated crucified.

We are regenerated crucified and are dying to live (1 Cor. 15:36). We were born dead, and now we are dying to live. *Dying to live* means to live under the crucifixion of Christ. Every day we are dying. Paul said that he died daily (1 Cor. 15:31; 2 Cor. 4:11). Our environment is putting us to death every day. Our dying is a continuous matter. The Christian life is a long life of dying. Every day we die to live. We were reborn crucified, and now we are dying to live. This is a living under the crucifixion of Christ. In Galatians 2:20, Paul said, "I am crucified with Christ; and it is no longer I who live, but it is Christ who lives in me; and the life which I now live in the flesh I live in faith...." On the one hand, Paul had been terminated, but on the other hand, a resurrected Paul, one who had been regenerated, still lived. Paul had been crucified with Christ, yet Christ lived in him and he lived Christ (Phil. 1:21a). Christ and Paul had one life and one living.

In the book *Born Crucified,* the writer tells a story that occurred during the Civil War in the United States. A man was chosen to go to the front to fight at the sacrifice of his life, yet he had a wife and six children. Another young man offered to go to replace this man, to be his substitute. Both parties agreed, and the authorities put this into their records. Then that young man who replaced the first man went to the

war and was killed in action. Later, the authorities still tried
to draft the first man into service. But the first man told
them to look at their records, which said that the other man
was his substitute. He claimed that he had died in the person
of the young man who was his substitute, his representative.
The author uses this case to illustrate that Christ was our
Substitute.

According to the legal record, this is a good illustration,
but according to the thought of our identification with Christ,
this illustration is inadequate. Christ was our Substitute on
the cross not just legally, to make a legal record in the heavenly account. He also came to be our Substitute in the way of
identification. First, He came into humanity. He did not come
to replace man but to be man. In the way of identification,
He came to become us. Spontaneously, He is our Substitute.

In the medical field, a doctor will give someone an injection at a spot on their body for the benefit of their entire body.
The doctor injects only one spot, but this one spot represents
the entire body, so the entire body receives the injection. This
spot where the injection takes place is not a kind of substitute
of our entire body in a legal way. This spot is a substitute for
the entire body in the way of identification. Thus, when this
spot receives the injection, the entire body receives it. Christ
could be our Substitute only in the way of identification. If He
had never become us, He could never have been our Substitute. If He had not become us, His being our Substitute would
have merely been according to a legal record. But because He
became us, His being our Substitute is according to the way of
identification.

Now we need to consider once more who died on the
cross. We need to say, "I died on the cross." When Christ was
incarnated, He took us upon Himself. He put on blood and
flesh (Heb. 2:14). Therefore, when He was crucified, we were
crucified with Him. All of us as a part of Christ, received the
injection of His death on the cross.

The writer of *Born Crucified* also told a story about an
old missionary who had lived a defeated Christian life. One
day he was reading the Bible, and his eyes fell upon the
words in Galatians 2:20—"Christ liveth in me." This phrase

enlightened that man. The book says that though he was a solid Presbyterian, he was jumping around his table with joy, saying, "Christ liveth in me! Christ liveth in me!" The Christ who lived in this Presbyterian missionary is the pneumatic Christ, the life-giving Christ.

Some may speak of the doctrine of identification, but they do not see that our identification with Christ can be experienced by us only in the life-giving Spirit. The Christ who was our Substitute became a life-giving Spirit (1 Cor. 15:45b). There are a number of people in Christianity who teach that the three of the Divine Trinity are three separate persons. To say this is wrong. There is no separation among the three, but there is a distinction among the Father and the Son and the Spirit. The three of the Godhead are one.

The New Testament says in 1 Corinthians 15:45b that the last Adam, who came to be our Substitute, became a life-giving Spirit. Christ as the last Adam became a life-giving Spirit for the purpose of indwelling us. If Christ as the God-man had never become the Spirit, how could He be our life within us? There would be no possibility of His dwelling in us if He were not the Spirit.

In Romans 8:9 Paul speaks of the Spirit of God dwelling in us and of our having the Spirit of Christ. Then in verse 10 he said, "If Christ is in you." "The Spirit of Christ" and "Christ" are interchangeably used. This means that the Spirit of Christ is Christ. These two titles refer to the same person. Second Corinthians 3:17 says, "The Lord is the Spirit." Then verse 18 speaks of "the Lord Spirit." This shows that the Lord Christ is the Spirit and the Spirit is the Lord Christ. First Corinthians 6:17 says, "He who is joined to the Lord is one spirit." How can we be identified with Christ? There is no way but in the life-giving Spirit.

Furthermore, in the Lord's revelation to us in His recovery, He has gone further to show us that this life-giving Spirit is the compound Spirit, compounded with Christ's divinity, with Christ's humanity, with Christ's human living, with Christ's death, with the effectiveness of Christ's death, with Christ's resurrection, and with the power of Christ's resurrection (see Philippians 1:19 and note 19[4]). Thus, He is the compound Spirit. Since we have such a compounded Spirit, we lack nothing. In Him we have God, the uplifted humanity, Christ's death, the effectiveness of His death, Christ's resurrection, and the power of His resurrection. Everything we need is here. We have to realize that in this pneumatic Christ, the life-giving Spirit, the compound Spirit, the death of Christ is available to us every day.

In these messages we are not burdened to merely teach the Bible. We want to expound all these things so that we would realize that the Spirit whom we are enjoying every day is a compound Spirit. This may be likened to a "compound" tea. When we drink the tea, we receive the elements of lemon, tea, and water since they have been compounded together. Similarly, as we drink the Spirit (1 Cor. 12:13b), we receive all of His elements, which include the death of Christ with its effectiveness and the resurrection of Christ with its power. Thus, as we are drinking the Spirit, we are dying to live. In the next message, we will continue our fellowship on our need to live and walk under the crucifixion of Christ.

CHAPTER THIRTEEN

LIVING AND WALKING
UNDER THE CRUCIFIXION OF CHRIST

(2)

Scripture Reading: Matt. 16:24-26; Gal. 5:24; Rom. 6:6; 8:13b

In the previous message we covered the matters of being regenerated crucified and of dying to live. The term *regenerated crucified* may seem strange, because the two words *regenerate* and *crucify* have opposite denotations. However, if we are regenerated, we are crucified. In our first birth there was no crucifixion. In that birth we were born to live. But in our second birth, that is, in regeneration, we were born crucified. We have been born, or regenerated, crucified. After being regenerated crucified, we continue to die.

After our baptism, every day we should live a dying life. Such a life is a continuation of our baptism. We should not forget that we are dead persons. Not only so, we should not forget that we are even buried persons. We are dead and we are buried. After our baptism we are dying. Every day we are dead persons, and now we live by dying.

In the phrase *regenerated crucified and dying to live* the conjunction *and* conjoins *regenerated* and *dying*. We are regenerated, and we are dying. We have been regenerated crucified, and now we need to die that we may live. After our baptism we live by dying and we die to live. Dying to live is the proper meaning of bearing the cross. From my youth I heard the teaching concerning bearing the cross. This teaching was based on the Lord's word in Matthew 16:24: "If anyone wants to come after Me, let him deny himself and take up his cross and follow Me." However, the understanding of many Christians concerning bearing the cross is not logical. According to their understanding, to bear the cross is to suffer. Because of this wrong understanding I wrote a hymn (*Hymns,* #622) concerning the meaning of the cross. The first stanza of that hymn says:

> If we take up the cross, will we but suffer pain?
> Nay, if we bear the cross, be sure that we will die!
> The meaning of the cross is that we may be slain;
> The cross experienced the self will crucify.

In the well-known book *Imitation of Christ,* the writer, considered by many to be Thomas à Kempis, taught that the way to perfection was to suffer with Christ. The teaching in that book is very close to the teaching of asceticism, which is taught strongly by Buddhism, by the Gnostics, and by the so-called Christian mystics, including Madame Guyon, Father Fenelon, and Brother Lawrence. Much of the teaching concerning bearing the cross is actually a form of asceticism. However, in Colossians 2:20-23 Paul spoke strongly against asceticism.

The teaching of asceticism seemingly has some ground in the Scriptures, for in 1 Peter 4:1, Peter said, "Since Christ therefore has suffered in the flesh, you also arm yourselves with the same mind (because he who has suffered in the flesh has ceased from sin)." In a sense, suffering does restrict people from sinning. When people are in poverty, they must work hard to earn a living, and they are restricted in their lusts. However, when people are wealthy, the amusements and the entertainments they pursue promote their lusts. If there were no truth to this, no one could have invented asceticism. Asceticism was invented by those who found out that when people become rich, they are often corrupted. The wrong teaching concerning bearing the cross is a form of asceticism.

The main concept of the book *Imitation of Christ* is erroneous. The Christian life is not an imitation of Christ but a participation in Christ. No one can imitate Christ, just as a monkey cannot imitate a man. We are fallen creatures. Sin has become our constitution. Every member of our body is a part of this sinful constitution. In Romans 7 Paul said that he had been sold under sin (v. 14). One who is sold under sin is a slave of sin. How can such a one be asked to keep the law? It is ridiculous to ask a slave of sin, one who is sold under sin, to keep the law.

The last of the Ten Commandments says, "Thou shalt not covet" (Exo. 20:17). This commandment is not related to outward conduct, but rather to the sin within man, mainly in his thoughts. Who can avoid coveting? Even a billionaire cannot avoid coveting. In Philippians 3 Paul said that as to the righteousness which is in the law, he had become blameless (v. 6). However, in Romans 7 Paul admitted that he was guilty of coveting (v. 7). Thus, Paul's boasting concerning his own righteousness is similar to David's boasting of his integrity in the Psalms (7:8; 26:1, 11; 41:12). Although Paul and David might have considered themselves righteous according to the law, at least for a certain time they were not righteous, for Paul coveted, and David murdered Uriah and robbed him of his wife, Bathsheba (2 Sam. 11), by this one act transgressing all the last five commandments in the law concerning man's conduct toward his fellow man (Exo. 20:13-17).

David is appreciated by many Jews and Christians. However, David committed a gross sin, and the remembrance of that sin remained long after David confessed it to God (Psa. 51). Even in the genealogy of Christ in Matthew, that sin of David's is mentioned (Matt. 1:6). In a sense Paul was good; even before he was a Christian he strove to keep the law. But in Romans 7 he told us that he did not succeed. In verse 9 he said that he was alive without the law once; but when the commandment came, sin revived and he died.

To bear the cross means, first, that Christ has brought us to the cross and, second, that we were crucified with Him on the cross (Gal. 2:20a). Since Christ was crucified and we were crucified in Him, we should see and should not forget that from that time a cross has been on our shoulder. When I was young I had very little awareness that a cross was upon me. However, especially in these past few years, the more I go along with the Lord, the more I feel that a cross is upon me. When I was a young Christian, I was quite free to argue with others. If I wanted to go to play a certain sport, I simply went to play. But today, especially in these past few years, a heavier cross has been upon me. Often when I want to do a certain thing, the Lord's answer within me is "no." That "no" is the cross. If you will check with your experience, you will admit that immediately after you were saved, in the first year of your Christian life, it was easy for you to get permission from the Lord Jesus to do certain things. Actually, the Lord Jesus did not give you the permission; it was you who gave yourself the permission. Then, after much growth in the Lord, the more you followed the Lord Jesus, the more you received the answer "no" when you sought the Lord's permission. You might ask the Lord if you can speak to a certain brother, and the Lord might say, "No! I want you to read the Bible." Then you might ask the Lord if you can go to sleep, but deep within you know that what the Lord wants you to do is to kneel down and pray. You would never propose that to the Lord. If you asked the Lord if He would like you to pray for an hour, He would surely say yes. Actually, there is no need for Him to say yes; you know deep within that that is what He wants you to do. However, you do not like to pray. Eventually, you agree with your own proposal, and thus you become the lord. At such a time there is no cross upon you. You have thrown the cross off your shoulder. That is not to bear the cross.

In my early ministry I was not free from the teaching of asceticism. At times I told the brothers that when they got married, they received a big cross, and that cross was their wife. I also told them that just one big cross was not adequate. Hence, after two years the Lord added a smaller cross, that is, a daughter. After another three years the Lord added another cross—a naughty son. That was my speaking in my earlier ministry. But today I would say that in the whole universe there is only one cross that can save us. This cross is not our cross but the cross of Christ. However, in Matthew 16 the Lord said that we must take up our own cross. This means that we must make the cross of Christ our cross. We were put on that cross already, and that cross was put on us. When we went to the baptistry to be baptized, we testified that we desired to take the way of the cross. We confessed that we had been crucified, crossed out, by the cross of Christ. After such a baptism, we need to be a person who bears the cross continually. The cross simply means that we have been put to death, and now we still need to be under that death. We need to realize that today we are not a living person but a dying person, and we have died already. The cross is upon us.

The first stanza of *Hymns,* #622 says that the meaning of the cross is not to suffer; rather, the meaning of the cross is to terminate our self. If we are living, actually, we are dying. On the other hand, if we are dying, in reality, we live. The apostle Paul taught this in Romans 8:13: "For if you live according to the flesh, you must die, but if by the Spirit you put to death the practices of the body, you will live." If we still live in our flesh, we must die, but if we bear the cross by dying throughout the day, we will live.

BEARING THE CROSS OF CHRIST AS OUR CROSS IN DEALING WITH OUR SOUL-LIFE—OUR SELF

We need to bear the cross of Christ as our cross in dealing with our soul-life, that is, our self (Matt. 16:24-26; Luke 9:23-25). The most difficult thing for us to deal with is not sin in our body but our self in our soul. The brothers who have been in the eldership for some time have found out that the most difficult thing in the church life is to deal with certain saints in their disposition. Likewise, the most difficult thing for a wife to deal with is her husband. It seems that a wife can deal with anything, but not with her husband's character and disposition. The more a wife lives with her husband, the more she finds out that her husband, with his disposition, his character, and his being, is a problem to her. This is the trouble that creates first a separation and then a divorce. The reason why there are so many separations and divorces today in America is that every American desires to be free; every American claims freedom as his human, civil right. This indicates that in a country such as the United States, which is full of Christians, very few people are living under the cross. Very few are dying under the cross; instead, most people are very living and very active in the flesh. It is very difficult for two people who are still living and active to remain together. The Bible teaches not only obedience but also submission

(Heb. 13:17; Eph. 5:21-22; Rom. 13:1). Everyone must submit to someone. To teach that there is no deputy authority is a serious error. Under God's divine administration, there is layer upon layer of deputy authority. If there is no submission, there is no cross.

At a certain point the Lord Jesus turned to His disciples and said, "If anyone wants to come after Me, let him deny himself and take up his cross and follow Me." In the universe there is an economy. According to God's economy, first He created mankind (Gen. 1:26-28). God created all the living creatures after their own kind (Gen. 1:21, 24-25). Then He created man in His image and after His likeness; that is, He created man after His kind. Man was created after God's kind, but God's intention in creating man was not to use the natural man. His intention was to use Himself within this man. Therefore, this man has to die so that God can live in this man. The created man should die so that the creating God can live within the created man. This is accomplished by the created man dying so that the creating God can enter into the created man to raise him up from his death. This is resurrection, and this is regeneration. The regenerated man is a living being with two natures, the human nature and the divine nature, and with two lives, the human life and the divine life. The natural nature and the natural life die, and man's second nature, his second life, lives. This kind of living is God living in the living of the second nature and the second life in resurrection. This is God's economy. The Christian life is a life of dying and living, a life in which the natural man dies and God lives in the resurrected man.

If this matter is not clear to us, we may make many mistakes. We need to see the basic principle and the basic factor of God's economy. We need to realize that when we were baptized, we were all buried in our baptistry. Therefore, we should remain in the baptistry, resting, sleeping, and dying there. That death is not a quick death. In man's eyes dying is nearly instantaneous, but in God's eyes dying takes a long time. We were all buried with Christ in His tomb (Rom. 6:4). That was the beginning of our dying. The dying that began in Christ's tomb has continued for the past twenty centuries. Today we are still dying. Whoever is not dying will be a troublemaker in the church life. If all the members of the church are dying and sleeping in their tomb, there will be no problems in the church life. All the problems in the church come from those who are still living.

The church life keeps us continually in the baptistry. To remain in the baptistry to die is to bear the cross. To bear the cross is to deal with us, the person—the Chinese person, the Mexican person, the American person, the German person. The cross deals with our being; it deals with what we are. This is to deal with the soul. However, many believers, after being saved for ten or twenty years, have never allowed their being to be touched by the Lord. It is impossible for such believers to experience any growth in life. As long as we live and do not die, we cannot grow. To grow means to have the Lord added into us (Col. 2:19). Merely believing in the Lord is not adequate; we need to experience the Lord's adding Himself into us. However, it is difficult for the Lord to add Himself into us because we are too strong and too full. Every inch of space in our being is ours; it is not Christ's. Thus, there is very little opportunity for the Lord to add Himself into us, and consequently there is very little growth in life. Growth in life is always in resurrection, and resurrection cannot come without crucifixion. Crucifixion is the threshold of resurrection. Once we enter into crucifixion, we will reach resurrection. In resurrection we enjoy Christ living in us. In resurrection Christ lives not only in us but also with us, and not only with us but also one with us. He makes Himself one with us.

According to God's eternal economy we, the created creatures, should die so that God can come in to raise us up, that we may live with God and God may live one with us, that is, in a way that makes Him and us one. First Corinthians 6:17 says, "But he who is joined to the Lord is one spirit." Such a spirit mentioned in this verse is the resurrection. One spirit means one resurrection, for in resurrection the Spirit of Christ equals the resurrection of Christ. In resurrection these two are one. Now all this has been transfused into our being; but we still insist on remaining in the old man. We still insist on living by our self in the old man. Thus, it is impossible for us to have a Christian life. On this earth it is difficult to see one person who is living a Christian life. We can see Christianity, but we cannot see a proper, genuine, Christian life. A proper and genuine Christian life is a life in which the created man dies so that God, the Creator, can come in to live with this one who has died, to live with him as one. This is altogether in resurrection. Here we can realize the Christian life. This is why in the four Gospels the Lord stressed the matter of bearing the cross very much. We need to bear our cross to remain in the death that has been allotted to us. In our human life, in our natural life, we are good for nothing (Rom. 7:18). Thus, God would not give us anything but would assign to us a death. We must remain there. If we remain in this death, we will be brought into resurrection, and in resurrection we will live God and He will live in us and with us; He will even live one with us. This is the Christian life.

CRUCIFYING OUR FLESH WITH ITS PASSIONS AND ITS LUSTS IN DEALING WITH OUR BODY OF SIN

Man is a tripartite being—spirit, soul, and body (1 Thes. 5:23). According to the fact in the Bible, although God has condemned sinful man and Satan has corrupted man, in God's economy, God has drawn a boundary around our spirit so that Satan cannot enter into our spirit. Satan can corrupt our body and our soul, but God has restricted Satan's corrupting to these two parts of our being and has reserved our spirit for Himself. When God enters into us, He enters into our spirit. Satan came in to corrupt our soul and our body. In the garden of Eden the serpent came to corrupt both Eve and Adam (Gen. 3:1-7). First he corrupted their soul, their mind; then their taking the fruit of the tree of knowledge corrupted their body. Sin was brought into the body, making the body the flesh, full of lusts and full of passions. But the spirit was preserved by God. Thus, there is still the possibility for us to repent. Repentance originates in one part of the spirit, that is, the conscience. The best way to preach the gospel is to stir up people's conscience so that they realize that they are sinful before God. Based on such a realization, they can repent. Repentance initiates from our conscience, and our conscience is a part of our spirit. Because of the existence of the conscience in man's spirit, the Chinese philosophers said that within human beings there is a part that they called "the bright virtue." In their logic they discovered that there is a part in fallen man that is reserved for God's use.

The Lord Jesus told us that we must bear the cross to deal with our soul, our self (Matt. 16:24-26; Luke 9:23-25). Then Paul said that he was crucified with Christ (Gal. 2:20a). No one can crucify himself. To be crucified one needs others to help him. It is possible for a person to commit suicide by many means, but no one can commit suicide by crucifixion, because no one can crucify himself. Yet, Galatians 5:24 says, "But they who are of Christ Jesus have crucified the flesh with its passions and its lusts." Although we cannot crucify ourselves, we can crucify our flesh, our fallen body, with its passions and its lusts. This is to deal with the body of sin. In Romans 6:6 Paul wrote, "Knowing this, that our old man has been crucified with Him in order that the body of sin might be annulled [or, unemployed, jobless, inactive]." Then in Galatians 5:24 Paul said that we must crucify our flesh. This corresponds with Romans 8:13, which says, "For if you live according to the flesh, you must die, but if by the Spirit you put to death the practices of the body, you will live." If we by the indwelling Spirit put to death the practices of our fallen body, we will not only live, but the divine life will also be transfused into our mortal body (Rom. 8:11). Here is the victory over sin. Our victory over sin is not that we are able to conquer sin; our victory over sin is in our remaining under the cross. Through the entire day, by our regenerated spirit with the help of the indwelling Spirit, we need to exercise Christ's crucifixion upon our flesh with its passions and its lusts.

Paul's word in Galatians 5:24 indicates that within our fallen flesh, which is the body of sin, there are two categories of things. The first category is our desires, or our passions. The second category is our lusts, that is, our evil desires that issue in evil actions. First, we have our desires; then the desires usher us into lusts. Thus, lusts are worse than desires, or passions. We need to crucify these two categories of things in our fallen flesh. First, we need to crucify our fleshly desires; then we need to crucify our fleshly evils, that is, our lusts.

In the Gospels, Matthew 16:24 tells us that we must bear the cross; that is, we must keep the death of Christ on our self, on our soul, continually. Then in the Epistles we are told that we must continually crucify our fleshly desires and lusts by our exercised spirit with the Holy Spirit, the indwelling Spirit, as a great help. Galatians 5:16 and 25 tell us to walk by the Spirit and to live by the Spirit. Then we must crucify our flesh with its passions and its lusts, which means that we must put all the practices of the body to death. Because we are still fallen, we cannot do this by ourselves; we must do it by the indwelling Spirit. There is another One who is indwelling us. The consummated God lives in us as the Spirit, and we have an organ, our spirit, that was preserved and is even indwelt by God. Hence, we should not remain in our flesh. Rather, we must come back from our flesh to our spirit. We must exercise our spirit; then the indwelling Spirit will help us to put Christ's death all the time on our flesh and on our fleshly passions and fleshly lusts. In this way we will kill all the means, all the organs, of sin. Sin will be jobless, and we will be freed from sin. Thus, these two things—dealing with our soul and dealing with our fleshly body—are both by the cross. To deal with our soul, we must bear the death of Christ, not allowing our self to live. We should always remind our self that the baptistry is a tomb where it was buried and where it should remain. This is to put the cross upon us, and this is to bear the cross. Furthermore, every day we need to exercise our spirit with the help of the indwelling Spirit to put every part of our flesh to death. Then our soul and our sinful body will be terminated. This is the way to live a victorious Christian life, and this is the Christian life.

If we practice these two things, no doubt, we will be in resurrection, and in resurrection we will enjoy the very God as the consummated Spirit, who is the pneumatic Christ as the embodiment of the processed Triune God. This is the economy of God.

CHAPTER FOURTEEN

LIVING AND WALKING
UNDER THE CRUCIFIXION OF CHRIST

(3)

Scripture Reading: John 3:5; Gal. 2:20a; 1 Cor. 15:36; Matt. 16:24-26; Gal. 5:24; Rom. 6:6; 8:13b; 2 Cor. 4:10, 16; Phil. 3:10

In message twelve we saw that we were regenerated crucified, born crucified (John 3:5; Gal. 2:20a), and that now we are dying to live (1 Cor. 15:36). In message thirteen we saw that we need to bear the cross of Christ as our cross in dealing with our soul-life, our self (Matt. 16:24-26), and that we need to crucify our flesh with its passions and lusts in dealing with our body of sin (Gal. 5:24; Rom. 6:6; 8:13b). In this message we want to see something further concerning our need to live and walk under the crucifixion of Christ.

UNDER THE KILLING OF CHRIST'S DEATH
THAT HIS LIFE MAY BE MANIFESTED IN OUR BODY
IN THE RENEWING OF THE INNER MAN

In the Christian life we are under the killing of Christ's death, and this has a purpose. The purpose is that His life may be manifested in our body in the renewing of the inner man (2 Cor. 4:10, 16). Second Corinthians 4 is concerning the renewing of our inner man.

As regenerated believers, we are complicated persons. We were born in the physical realm, and then we were regenerated in the spiritual realm. We have had two births, so we are a "double person." By our natural birth we are an old man. Even though a person is only nineteen years old, he is still an old man. Through regeneration, through the second birth, we all became a new man. Now outwardly we are old, but inwardly we are new. However, God is not satisfied to leave us in the old man. He wants our old man to be renewed by transformation. Transformation transfers us from one form, the form of the old man, to another form, the form of the new man. The word *transform* means to be transferred to another form. The Lord accomplishes this by the killing of Christ's death.

In message twelve we pointed out that we were born crucified, regenerated crucified. Thus, from the day of our regeneration, we have been a dying person. In one sense, we are living, but in another sense, we are dying. We are dying to live (1 Cor. 15:36). If there is no death, there is no life. If we do not die, we cannot live.

In 2 Corinthians 4:10 Paul said we are "always bearing about in the body the putting to death of Jesus." *Putting to death* here means *killing*. The death of Christ kills us. His death is the killing capacity within us.

The Death of Christ
in the Compound Spirit

We should not forget that His death is included in the all-inclusive, compound Spirit. The Holy Spirit today is a compound Spirit, typified by the compound ointment in Exodus 30:23-25. This compound Spirit has God as the base, typified by one hin of olive oil. This oil is compounded with four spices—myrrh, cinnamon, calamus, and cassia. These spices typify the elements of Christ's death and resurrection. Furthermore, the number four typifies the created man. Thus, the Spirit, typified by the ointment, is a compound of God and man. The God-man, Jesus, has been compounded together with the elements of His death and resurrection.

In this compound Spirit, there is the death of Christ, and the death of Christ is active. Within today's antibiotics there is some element that is very active to kill the germs. In like manner, within this compound Spirit as a big dose, there is the element of Christ's death which is active in killing all the negative things within us.

The Killing of Christ's Death
through Our Environment

Second Corinthians 4:10 indicates that the death of Christ kills us. The apostle Paul always was under the killing of Christ's death. According to history and according to the biblical record, Paul became an apostle bearing the burden to spread God's economy through the preaching of the gospel. He was always under people's persecution. A number of people were trying to kill him. He was continually under the persecution of the Jews, the Gentiles, and the Judaizers. This is why Paul said that he died daily (1 Cor. 15:31). Daily he risked death, faced death, and died to self (2 Cor. 11:23; 4:11; 1:8-9; Rom. 8:36). He was bearing about in his body the killing of Jesus so that the life of Jesus could be manifested in him.

In such a one who was daily under the killing of Jesus, people saw Christ. For him to live was Christ, and to live Christ is to magnify Christ (Phil. 1:20-21a). Even when he was in a Roman prison, he did not want to be put to shame. To be put to shame, to shame the Lord, would mean that people could not see Christ in him. But Paul was not put to shame. Even when he was in prison, people saw Christ in him. The manifested Christ is the life which comes out of the killing of Christ. This is what it means to live and walk under the crucifixion of Christ.

We need to live Christ under the crucifixion of Christ, under the killing of Jesus' death. Some may feel that since they are not the apostle Paul and are not under the kind of persecution which he experienced, they do not experience this killing. However, all of us are under this killing to a certain extent. The Lord may want us to do something which is against our will. When we follow the Lord against our will, this is a killing.

All of the full-time trainees are being killed every day. To eat food and stay in dormitories against their choice is a killing. Under God's divine and sovereign arrangement, our entire environment is a killing. All the things in our environment are like knives to kill us. The wives, the husbands, the children, the brothers, and everything in our environment are used by the Lord as knives to kill us.

It is difficult to say whether we are enjoying the Lord or suffering in the Christian life. Sometimes we are in the "day" enjoying the Lord. At other times, our spiritual day is unclear with very little shining. Then there are times when it seems that we are suffering in the night. But we need to realize that the earth cannot exist without night. The earth can only exist with days and nights. According to the Bible, there is first the evening and then the morning (Gen. 1:5). The Bible starts from the night, but we start from the day.

We may think that the Christian life is always a pleasant, happy life. But this happy life does not exist by itself. If the Christian life were merely a happy life, the apostle Paul would not have needed to charge us to rejoice (Phil. 4:4). While we are suffering and wiping away our tears, we should rejoice. In order to weep, we do not need any kind of encouragement. Paul does not charge us to weep in the Lord, but he does charge us to rejoice in the Lord. If we do not exercise our spirit to rejoice in the midst of our killing environment, we cannot have any joy.

God in His sovereignty is putting us all the time under the killing of the cross. The apostle Paul was under the killing of the cross, and so are we. We do not experience as much suffering and persecution as he did, but we are still under this killing. This is God's divine arrangement.

In marriage life, both the husband and the wife experience being killed. I encourage all the young people to get married. To frustrate people from being married is a teaching of demons (1 Tim. 4:1-3). Marriage life, however, is a suffering. A sister can be a very good wife, yet she is also a killing factor to her husband. The husbands are also the killing factors to the wives. When a person is single, he is still somewhat free, but when a person gets married, he enters into a cage. In marriage life, our freedom is taken away, and we suffer.

The killing of the cross, the killing of Christ's death, ushers in resurrection. When we are willing to suffer and be killed, we live Christ, we magnify Christ, and Christ is manifested in us. Then we are transformed. We enjoy Christ under the killing of His death. I see many of the saints smiling, and their smiling is the manifestation of Christ. They are smiling while they are under the killing of the cross. On the other hand, we Christians, at least to a certain extent, are hypocrites. A hypocrite is an actor with a false appearance, and this false appearance is a mask. We may wear a mask before others, but that mask is not the real person. Many times we are not so genuine. Instead, we are pretending. As we are under the killing of Christ's death, Christ as the genuine One needs to be manifested in us.

We have to realize that our circumstances and our environment are altogether not up to us. They are like the weather. Whether it is raining or whether the sky is clear is up to God, the Creator. He arranges all things, both big and small. This is why Paul said that all things work together for our good so that we can be conformed to the image of Christ (Rom. 8:28-29). Everything works for our good under God's arrangement through the killing of Christ's death. All day long we are under this killing. On the one hand, we are enjoying Christ, and on the other hand, we are under the killing of Christ's death. This is the Christian life.

Thus, our outer man is being consumed, but our inner man is being renewed day by day (2 Cor. 4:16). As our outer man is being consumed by the killing work of death, our inner man, that is, our regenerated spirit with the inward parts of our being, is being metabolically renewed day by day with the supply of the resurrection life. This is what it means to live and walk under the killing of Jesus, the crucifixion of Christ. The real Christian life is a life under the killing of Christ's death.

We may feel that no one would want to believe in the Lord Jesus if they realized that the Christian life is a life under such a killing. But our believing in the Lord Jesus is not up to us. If it had been up to us, none of us would have believed. The Lord is sovereign, and He managed everything in our life to bring us to believe in Him.

David said to the Lord, "My times are in Your hand" (Psa. 31:15a). *My times* means *my things.* Our birth, our believing in the Lord Jesus, and all the things through which we pass are not up to us. All of our things are in His hand. Actually, they are within Christ. This does not mean that we are so willing, but it does mean that He is sovereign. He arranges all things.

I was saved by the Lord after hearing a message in a large gospel meeting. While I was walking home from that meeting, I offered myself to God. I told Him that I would give up the whole world for Him and that I would be willing to travel throughout the villages to preach the gospel. Eventually, the Lord did not allow me to travel to the villages. Instead, I was brought to the big cities all the time.

Later, I had the intention of evangelizing the people of Inner Mongolia. Eventually, however, I did not end up in Inner Mongolia but in California. I surely realize that my times, my things, are not up to me. I never thought that I would be in the United States for the Lord's recovery. If our times were up to us, we would never be killed. The Lord's sovereignty is operating to put us under the killing of Christ's death.

Everything related to us is under the Lord's sovereign arrangement. What kind of job we have and whom we marry are altogether not up to us. A brother may choose a sister to be his wife, but later this brother may think that he made a mistake. This is why the Lord charges the husbands to love their wives (Eph. 5:25). Under the Lord's sovereign arrangement, we are like lambs brought to the slaughter every day (Rom. 8:36). Every day we are being slaughtered. Every day we are under the killing of Christ's death that His life may be manifested in our body in the renewing of our inner man.

CHAPTER FIFTEEN

LIVING AND WALKING
UNDER THE CRUCIFIXION OF CHRIST

(4)

Scripture Reading: John 3:5; Gal. 2:20a; 1 Cor. 15:36; Matt. 16:24-26; Gal. 5:24; Rom. 6:6; 8:13b; 2 Cor. 4:10, 16; Phil. 3:10

In this message we want to conclude our fellowship on our need to live and walk under the crucifixion of Christ.

BEING CONFORMED TO THE DEATH OF CHRIST
BY THE POWER OF HIS RESURRECTION
IN THE FELLOWSHIP OF HIS SUFFERINGS

In Philippians 3:10 the apostle Paul said that he desired to be conformed to the death of Christ by the power of His resurrection in the fellowship of His sufferings. Who can say what the conformation to the death of Christ and what the power of Christ's resurrection are? Christ's death and resurrection are great mysteries.

Recently, I received some news about a sister who passed through certain sufferings. If we consider the issues which she is facing in her spiritual life, this will help us to realize what it means to be conformed to the death of Christ. This sister was forced to resign from her job because the work she was doing had a harmful effect on her health. After her resignation, she considered that she should use some of her savings to start a business. She saw an advertisement in the newspaper from a man who was looking for an investor for his business. This sister and her husband were convinced by this man to invest their money in this business. They put all of their savings into that man's hands. Eventually, he cheated them and they lost all of their money.

As a result of what happened to her, this sister became very bothered. First, she wondered about the Lord's faithfulness. She said that for many years she prayed every day and honestly trusted in the Lord for everything. She wondered why the Lord did not help her since she had prayed so much and had so much trust in Him. She said that she had dedicated her time to study the Bible with the help of the life-studies and the books we have published. Since she gave herself to the Lord in this way, she wondered why the Lord did not do anything for her and why the Lord would not protect her. She lost her health, her job, and then her savings even though she had prayed and trusted the Lord.

She pointed out that in one of Brother Nee's books, he said that the Lord does not care whether we are successful or mistaken. What the Lord desires is to work Himself into us. She asked if this meant that the Lord wanted us to neglect all the practical matters and only take care of God's desire to work Himself into us. She said that she had been dedicating herself and her time to reading the Bible and the publications of the ministry every day. She was wondering how her spiritual seeking and her care for practical matters could be reconciled. It seemed to her that she trusted in the Lord to no avail. What could she tell her children about this? In this message I would like to address these issues.

Brother Nee was absolutely right in saying that God does not care whether we are successful or whether we are mistaken. God cares only for one thing—for being worked into us. God does not have any intention to make someone a great professor. There are flocks of scholars and professors on earth already. God's intention is not to build up a world full of professors. God's intention is to build up His kingdom. All who are in His kingdom must be those who give God the full ground and the full opportunity to work Himself into them. This is why Paul said in Romans 8:28 that all things work together for good to those who love God. What is the "good" about which Paul is speaking here? Is this "good" a high degree or a promotion?

If we love God, He will cause all things to work together for our good, but the good is not what we may want or expect. The good is what God intends to work out according to Romans 8. The good is for us to be conformed to the image of His firstborn Son (v. 29). God's heart's desire is not related to whether we get a good job or get promoted. He is not concerned about whether we make a lot of money or lose money. In fact, God may use all things to cause a person to lose money. If this person made money, God would have no chance to work Himself into that person. When a person loses money, he may complain to God, but God is taking this opportunity to dispense Himself into this person.

Many of us think we know how to pray, but actually we do not know how to pray in a fitting way. Paul indicated that the best prayer is to groan (Rom. 8:26, 23). We do not know how to pray, but the Spirit teaches us how to pray. The Spirit teaches us to groan. This sister wondered why she lost all her money. She trusted in the Lord so much, but the Lord did not lead her to the right person. Then she did not know how to pray. When we do not know how to pray, we groan. That is the best way to pray.

We have seen that in many of the psalms, David was clear about how to pray, and he even instructed God to fight against his enemies with weapons (Psa. 35:1-3). Of course, this kind of prayer is not according to God's way. We surely should not instruct God in our prayer. Especially, we should not tell Him to deal with our enemies, because this is against the teaching of the New Testament (Matt. 5:44).

We have seen in our life-study of the Psalms that the title of Psalm 34 says that David wrote this psalm after he had disguised himself in hypocrisy before Abimelech (see message sixteen of *Life-study of the Psalms*). David disguised himself to make Abimelech think that he was insane, and then he blessed and praised God for delivering him. Actually, he delivered himself by disguising himself, and then he gave God the credit.

Instead, David should have said, "Lord, what shall I pray?" If David had prayed in this way, he would have been spiritual. But David was so bold to bless and praise Jehovah for hearing him and delivering him. Actually, David practiced falsehood to cheat that king. Was that God's answering him? I am saying this to help us realize that when we are so clear about how to pray, this means we are natural and in ourselves. The best prayer many times is to say, "Lord, I don't know how or what to pray." We do not know the kind of prayer God desires, and we are not clear how to pray; hence we groan. In our groaning, the Spirit groans also, interceding for us. God the Father answers when the Spirit intercedes for us, and He arranges our circumstances, causing all things to work together for good to us.

God puts us into the right position so that we can be broken. Often God will not do anything for us according to our concept, and it may seem to us that God is not faithful. We may pray day and night and put our trust in the Lord, but eventually nothing comes out according to our earnest prayer. We may want to get a promotion on our job, but we may not get it. We may want to invest our savings to make some profit, but eventually we may lose money.

We should not spend or invest our money in a way that is not according to Christ. The Lord said that He sent us forth as sheep in the midst of wolves. Who is trustworthy on this earth? Most of the people are wolves. The Lord also said that we have to be prudent as serpents and guileless as doves (Matt. 10:16). As sheep in the midst of wolves, we have to be prudent as serpents to escape being hurt by the wolves, and guileless as doves, not mixed with any evil intention and not hurting others.

Many people who put advertisements in the newspaper saying that they need someone to invest money into their businesses are actually preparing a net to trap people. To trust in such persons is foolish. If we entrust our money to such persons and lose our money, how can we blame the Lord for not answering us and not doing anything for us? Actually, the Lord in His sovereignty may allow us to lose our money, but when every cent is gone, God is still here. We may complain to God, but our complaining may be the best prayer, the most pleasant prayer to God. While we are complaining, God is rejoicing because He is causing all things to work together for good that we may be conformed to the image of His firstborn Son.

Whether we make money or lose money means nothing to God. Actually, money, mammon, is the incarnation of the devil. We may wonder how we can eat if we do not care for mammon. But the Lord said that we cannot serve God and mammon and that if we seek God and His kingdom, God will care for our needs (Matt. 6:24, 33).

One day the disciples of the Pharisees and the Herodians came to test the Lord Jesus by asking Him whether they should pay taxes to Caesar or not. Then the Lord asked them to give Him a coin. This meant that the Lord Jesus did not have any money; instead they had it. The Lord asked them whose image was on the coin. When they said that it was Caesar's image, the Lord responded, "Render then the things that are Caesar's to Caesar and the things that are God's to God" (Matt. 22:21). The Lord Jesus did not have a Roman coin but asked them to show one to Him. Since they possessed one of the Roman coins, they were caught. Surely our Lord was free from the bondage of mammon. When the Lord said that we cannot serve God and mammon, this indicates that wealth or riches is the opponent of God, robbing God's people of their service to Him. To be free from the bondage of mammon to serve God is to live and walk under the crucifixion of Christ.

When Christ was living on this earth, He was under the killing of death every day. He refused to remain in any relationship in the natural life. This displayed His absoluteness for God in His humanity. When He was told that His mother, brothers, and sisters were seeking Him, He declared that those who do the will of God are His brother and sister and mother (Mark 3:31-35). Through His gospel service, the Slave-Savior made the believing sinners His spiritual relatives, who became His many brothers (Rom. 8:29; Heb. 2:11) in the house of God (Heb. 3:5-6) and His many members for the building up of His mystical Body (Eph. 5:30; 1 Cor. 12:12) to do the will of God.

Later when the Lord was on the cross, He saw His mother and His disciple John standing by, and He said to His mother, "Woman, behold, your son" (John 19:26). We should not forget that the Lord had the human nature and human feelings. For Him to be hanging on the cross and tell His mother not to look at Him but to look at John as her son was a death to the natural life.

Death is the threshold of resurrection. Whenever we enter into death, we should realize that we are on the threshold of resurrection. The sister who lost her job and her money could complain to God, but she could not forsake God. On the one hand, she was complaining to God, and on the other hand, she is still with God. At a certain point, she should be able to praise the Lord even though she lost all of her savings. She eventually should be able to declare to the universe that even though she does not have any savings, she is still living. She is living not on her savings but on her living God. The living God is resurrection. We are living by resurrection, not by any money which we have accumulated. When we do not have much money, we are released. Actually, people who have too much money are very burdened because they become anxious about losing it.

The parents need to consider what the difference is between having or not having children. Eventually, when we do the "mathematics" in the Spirit, we would say that it is about the same. On the one hand, we parents surely love our children, but on the other hand, our children cause us much trouble. Those who do not have any children do not have to experience this trouble. But God uses our children, the loss of our children, and even our not having children to break us that He might have the chance to work Himself into us.

As we are under the experience of the breaking of our outer man, we will learn to pray not by clear words. We would even tell the Lord that we do not know how to pray. Some saints are too bold to pray too much. They need to learn to groan according to Paul's word in Romans 8:26. Some sisters among us are female "psalmists." They have so much to pray and are so clear about what to pray. They need to learn to groan. Many times we do not know what to pray because we cannot figure out what is going on in our circumstances. We do know, however, that the apostle Paul said in Romans 8:28 that all things work together for our good.

Some of the brothers who come to me for fellowship tell me only the good things, not the bad things. But actually in the universe the night comes first and then the day (Gen. 1:5). If the news I get in my fellowship with the brothers is all in the "day," I am cheated in my realization of the real situation. If I know the real situation of the saints in the church, I can pray for them. But if I am told that everything is wonderful, everyone is practicing the new way, and everything is in the "day," I am not aware of the real situation. The Lord uses all things, both the things in the "day" and the things in the "night," to transform us and conform us to His image.

Only the Lord knows the heavenly, spiritual mathematics concerning what in our environment works the best for our good. The Lord gave Job many children, but one day all of his sons and daughters were killed (Job 1:18-19). Job prayed a good prayer by saying, "Naked I came out of my mother's womb, and naked I will return there. Jehovah gives and Jehovah takes away; blessed be the name of Jehovah" (vv. 20-22). This, however, is still not the best prayer, because it is an Old Testament prayer. A New Testament prayer would say, "Lord, thank You for giving me children and for taking away my children. Through Your giving and through Your taking away I have been transformed and filled up with You. The coming and going of my children are all Your doing to transform me and fill me up."

Children are used by God to deal with the parents. Some parents are dealt with by God mainly by their children. But God knows whether we need children or do not need children. He uses all things to conform us to the image of Christ. Some persons may be nice, gentle, and faithful in their natural man. They would be good persons even apart from being regenerated or transformed. Then what can God do to work Himself into such persons? With such persons and with all of us, God must put us into certain circumstances to break us. God's desire is for us to be broken so that He can work Himself into us.

Paul was a person who was conformed to the death of Christ by something mysterious called the power of resurrection. No one can be conformed to the death of Christ except by the resurrection power. There is something within us hidden, mysterious, and dynamic called resurrection. Eventually, we will learn that whether money comes or money goes, whether children come or children go, God remains. God is our portion. He is not our portion outwardly but our portion inwardly in the way of constitution. God has constituted and is constituting Himself into our being. Eventually, God uses all things to make Himself our unique portion.

Our money, our children, our job, and our degree are not our portion. Only God is our portion. Some of us have portions other than Christ Himself. We may have our own goals which we desire to reach, saying that we need to be practical. But actually these goals are our portion. This is why God comes to "peel off" our natural life layer by layer throughout the years. I have been under God's gradual "peeling" for almost seventy years. I am happy today because much of my natural life has been peeled off. God uses all things to "peel off" our natural life. God even uses all the brothers and sisters in the church life to accomplish this peeling. We are all under the accumulating process of God's "peeling off" of our natural life. The day will come when we will have a great and serious peeling off. Then we will be broken, "bankrupt." "Bankruptcy" means brokenness.

Some today teach positive thinking as the way to be successful in everything. Such a teaching is terrible and absolutely off. Did the apostle Paul practice positive thinking to be successful or to make money? Paul was positive in martyrdom. He was very positive in being ready to be poured out as a drink offering (Phil. 2:17; 2 Tim. 4:6).

I would encourage all of us to read the biography of Brother Watchman Nee (entitled *Watchman Nee: A Seer of the Divine Revelation in the Present Age* published by Living Stream Ministry). Brother Nee's ministry has spread throughout the world. Many seeking Christians have received help from his ministry. Eventually, however, he died in imprisonment. This is the conformation to the death of Christ. Within Brother Nee there was a mystery. That mystery within him was the power of resurrection.

After we have been under God's dealing for some time, we are so willing to be conformed to Christ's death in everything. To us Christians there should be no thought of revenge or avenging ourselves. We do not want to remember others' mistakes. To forgive and forget others' mistakes is the conformation to the death of Christ. We do not like to blame others. When we blame others, regardless of how right we are, we do not have the peace.

We want to be conformed to the death of Christ, and we can be such persons only by the hidden power of resurrection. We cannot see this hidden power in David in many of the psalms. In many of the psalms, David was strong in remembering others' mistakes. He even enumerated to God all the afflictions and mistreatment he suffered from his enemies and asked God to deal with them (Psa. 31:9-13; 35:1-8; 36:1-4, 11-12).

If we would go to the Lord to tell Him all the mistreatment we suffered from our enemies, we would become dead inside. Instead, we have to follow the Lord's word where He said, "You have heard that it was said, `You shall love your neighbor and hate your enemy.' But I say to you, Love your enemies, and pray for those who persecute you, so that you may become sons of your Father who is in the heavens, because He causes His sun to rise on the evil and the good and sends rain on the just and the unjust. For if you love those who love you, what reward do you have? Do not even the tax collectors do the same? And if you greet only your brothers, what better thing are you doing? Do not even the Gentiles do the same? You therefore shall be perfect as your heavenly Father is perfect" (Matt. 5:43-48). We can be perfect like our Father because we have been born of Him. We have His life and His nature. This is the New Testament teaching.

Today we are mysterious people. Outsiders cannot understand us because we have a desire to be conformed to Christ's death. Furthermore, we have the capacity within us to do this, and this capacity is the power of resurrection. Even nature itself testifies to the fact of resurrection. Within a small seed there is not only life but also resurrection. If that seed falls into the earth and dies, a sprout will eventually rise up from underneath the earth. That is the power of resurrection. We are like small seeds. The more we are put into death, the more we have the expression of the power of resurrection. This is why we like to forgive people and forget their mistakes.

In a proper sense, we want to suffer loss so that we can gain Christ (Phil. 3:7-8). There are some hymns in our hymnal which speak about loss and gain (see *Hymns*, #631 and #635—stanzas 15 and 16). Loss and gain is the significance of the cross. The cross is a means to bring us loss and then gain. To live and walk under the crucifixion of Christ is to be conformed to Christ's death by the mysterious power of resurrection. Just as life and resurrection are hidden within a seed, Christ as life and resurrection is hidden within us. Within us we have Christ as our life and resurrection.

As we are being conformed to the death of Christ, we are in the fellowship of His sufferings. We are a real partner, a real companion, of the Lord in His sufferings. During the Lord's life on this earth, He did not have any peace in His environment. Every day He was suffering, so Isaiah refers to Him as a man of sorrows (Isa. 53:3). The apostle Paul was also a man without any peace in his environment. No doubt, Paul was conformed to the death of Christ by the inner, hidden, mysterious power of resurrection.

Some Pentecostals think you have to wait and pray for three days, and then suddenly you will receive power. This is a wrong concept about power. The real power is within us. How can this power be expressed? It can be expressed by our being conformed to Christ's death. When we are being conformed to His death, power comes out. Then we are a companion, a partner, of the Lord in His sufferings. This means that we are in the fellowship of the Lord's sufferings.

No matter what our circumstances are, we are still living, so we have to worship the Lord. We should tell the Lord, "Lord, as long as I am living on this earth, I am much blessed because while I am living, You have the opportunity to work Yourself increasingly into my being, to constitute my being with Your element."

Through our sufferings, we have the opportunity to gain more of God. Eventually, after passing through many sufferings, we have more of God in us. As long as we have more of God, this is what really matters. Whether or not we have a good promotion or whether or not we make money does not make any difference. Instead, all the losses become the increase of God in us. Therefore, we have to praise Him.

CHAPTER SIXTEEN

CONFORMED TO THE DEATH OF CHRIST

Scripture Reading: Rom. 6:6; Eph. 4:22, 24; 2 Cor. 4:16; Rom. 8:13b; 2 Cor. 4:10; Phil. 3:10b

In this message I would like to help you to see another aspect of the Christian life, the aspect of being conformed to the death of Christ. Many Christians are unfamiliar with this phrase in the Bible. However, the Lord has shown us this matter through the past seventy years, beginning with Brother Nee. Brother Nee began to minister in 1922, when he was just nineteen years old. Later in that same year the first local church was established in his home town of Foochow. Approximately ten years later I joined Brother Nee in the work, and I began to learn of him and to practice under him. Then, in 1949 I was sent by him from mainland China to Taiwan. Three years later, in 1952, Brother Nee was put into prison; that terminated his personal ministry among us. For the eighteen years that I was with him, I spoke very few messages that were not directly from his teaching. What Brother Nee taught, I taught. This was known among us for many years.

Then I went to Taiwan and began to work seemingly apart from him, because he was on the mainland and I was on the island of Taiwan. For the first two or three years my ministry remained in the sphere of what Brother Nee had taught, but shortly after 1950 the Lord began to show me something further. This has continued until today, for more than forty years.

In 1962 I came to the United States and began the work of the Lord's recovery in this country. During the past thirty years there has been even further progress in the seeing of the divine revelation. On mainland China we did not emphasize the term *economy*. Instead of the word *economy*, Brother Nee used the word *plan*. In his books he used the term *God's eternal plan;* he never used the word *economy*. After coming to the United States, I did not have the thought of God's economy until 1964. In that year I spoke the messages published in the book *The Economy of God*. It was at that time that I began to use the word *economy*, which is the anglicized form of the Greek word *oikonomia*. Later, beginning from 1984, I began to stress God's dispensing for the accomplishment of God's economy. In 1990 I spoke strongly on the divine economy and the divine dispensing (see *A Deeper Study of the Divine Dispensing, The Economy and Dispensing of God,* and *The Divine Dispensing for the Divine Economy,* published by Living Stream Ministry). I say this to illustrate how the Lord has shown us the divine things in a progressive way.

THE OLD MAN AND THE NEW MAN OF A BELIEVER

As believers we all have our old man and also the new man (Rom. 6:6; Eph. 4:22, 24). We also can say that we believers of Christ *are* both the old man and the new man. In Romans 6:6 Paul said that our old man has been crucified with Christ. Then, in Ephesians 4:22, 24 he said that we need to put off the old man and put on the new man. Such a thing has not been thoroughly taught in today's Christianity, but in the Lord's recovery this has been ministered to the saints throughout the past sixty-eight years. In 1924 Brother Nee began to speak concerning the old man and the new man. In his book *The Spiritual Man* he made this matter more than clear. If we check with our experience, we will realize that at times we are the new man, and at other times we are the old man. Thus, we are both the old man and the new man. After our morning revival we are the new man, but a short time later we may be offended by someone and become the old man. Then, after repenting and confessing our failure to obtain the Lord's forgiveness, we become the new man again. This kind of experience is the story of our Christian life. The Christian life is a life in which we are sometimes the old man and at other times the new man.

OUR OLD MAN (THE OUTER MAN) TO BE CONSUMED, BUT OUR NEW MAN (THE INNER MAN) TO BE RENEWED DAY BY DAY

God's economy is to have our old man (the outer man) consumed and our new man (the inner man) renewed day by day (2 Cor. 4:16). Being consumed is not the same as being killed. A person may be killed instantly, but the consuming of our old man is a long process that requires many years. I have been in this process for nearly seventy years; nevertheless, the consuming of my old man has not yet been consummated.

Every day in the church life we are being consumed. This consuming is our being molded, or conformed, to the death of Christ (Phil. 3:10c). In making cakes, dough is put into a mold and pressed into the mold. In this way the dough is conformed to the form of the mold. If the mold is in the image of a fish, the dough that is pressed into this mold will be conformed to the shape of a fish. The death of Christ is our mold, and we are the dough. Since the day we were saved, we became the dough. This dough is made of fine flour from wheat (Lev. 2:1; John 12:24; 1 Cor. 10:17). Christ is the fine flour for us to be made the dough.

God has put us all into the mold of Christ's death. The death to which we are being conformed is not Adam's death but Christ's death. The death of Christ is a particular death. Out of millions and even billions of deaths, only Christ's death is a particular death. From the time that we became dough, God put us into this death (Rom. 6:4), considering this death as a mold. Day by day and year after year God is molding us to conform us to this death.

On the one hand, we are happy in the recovery and in the church life, but on the other hand, deep within we are suffering here. However, we have no way to escape. Every day we are being molded. When we come to the dining table to eat, we may not like the food that has been prepared for us. This is part of the mold, the mold of the death of Christ. Marriage too is a part of this mold. Marriage is used very much by the Lord to conform the married ones to the death of Christ.

THROUGH OUR PUTTING TO DEATH
THE PRACTICES OF OUR BODY BY THE SPIRIT

According to Romans 8:13, we are conformed to the death of Christ through our putting to death the practices of our body by the Spirit. It is not the body itself but its practices that we must put to death. The body needs to be redeemed (v. 23), but its practices need to be put to death. These practices include not only sinful things but also all things practiced by our body apart from the Spirit.

We must put to death the practices of the body, but we must do it by the Spirit. On the one hand, we must take the initiative to put to death the practices of the body; the Spirit does not do it for us. On the other hand, we should not attempt to deal with our body by relying on our own effort without the power of the Holy Spirit.

The putting to death here is actually our coordinating with the Spirit who indwells us. Inwardly, we must allow Him to make His home in us that He may give life to our mortal body (v. 11). Outwardly, we must put to death the practices of our body that we may live. When we take the initiative to put to death the practices of our body, the Spirit comes in to apply the effectiveness of Christ's death to those practices, thus killing them.

BEARING ABOUT THE PUTTING TO DEATH OF JESUS
THAT THE LIFE OF JESUS ALSO MAY BE MANIFESTED

We are conformed to the death of Christ by bearing about in the body the putting to death of Jesus that the life of Jesus also may be manifested in our body (2 Cor. 4:10). The putting to death of Jesus refers to the working of death, the working of the cross, which the Lord Jesus suffered and went through. In our experience this is a kind of suffering, persecution, or dealing that comes upon us for the sake of Jesus, for the sake of the Body of Christ, and for the sake of the new covenant ministry. This does not refer to sufferings and troubles that are common to all human beings in the old creation, such as illness or calamity, or to punishment, correction, or discipline suffered because of sins, mistakes, or failure to fulfill one's responsibility. This putting to death of Jesus consumes our natural man, our outward man, our flesh, so that our inward man may have the opportunity to develop and be renewed (v. 16). The experience of the putting to death of Jesus results in the manifestation of the life of Jesus in our body. The life of Jesus here is the resurrection life, which the Lord Jesus lived and expressed through the working of the cross.

IN THE FELLOWSHIP OF THE SUFFERINGS OF CHRIST

Christ's death did not take place only in the six hours of His crucifixion. Christ's death began from His birth and continued to His last breath while He was on the cross. Therefore, the death of Christ was a process that lasted thirty-three and a half years. First, after Christ was born, He was not placed in a comfortable home but was laid in a manger (Luke 2:7). A short time later Herod attempted to kill Him (Matt. 2:7-12, 16-18). Then He escaped to Egypt and became an escapee there (vv. 13-15). Later, His parents wanted to bring Him back to Judea, but because Archelaus the son of Herod was reigning over Judea, Mary and Joseph were afraid to stay there, so they took Jesus and settled in the despised city of Nazareth in the despised region of Galilee (vv. 19-23). There the Lord lived not in a mansion but in a carpenter's cottage. Although Mary, His mother, was very spiritual and knew the Scriptures very well (Luke 1:46-55), at times even she troubled the Lord Jesus (John 2:3-4). Through this we can see that every day and even every minute of those thirty-three and a half years, Christ was dying.

The death of Christ was the aggregate of all His sufferings. We are not the only ones who are being consumed; Christ took the lead to be consumed. From the time that He was born, He was under the consuming. This consuming was His sufferings, and the totality of His sufferings equals His death. Thus, Christ's death took place over a period of thirty-three and a half years. The death with the greatest suffering is the death that occurs over a long period of time. Christ's death was such a suffering death. We, His believers, are in the fellowship of His sufferings (Phil. 3:10b). To be in the fellowship of Christ's sufferings is to participate in Christ's sufferings.

The reason for Christ's death is twofold. First, Christ came to do the will of the Father (Heb. 10:7-9a). Whenever we do the will of God, the entire world, including Satan, men, and even the demons, will oppose us (John 15:18-19). Because we are people who are doing the will of God, every day we suffer. The Christian life is not a life of pleasures. On the contrary, the Christian life is a life of suffering because we are doing the will of God.

Today there is some division in the Lord's recovery. Some of the dear ones who are with us are making divisions. Because of the contagious germs of division within these ones, it is not wise for us to contact them. According to Romans 16:17 and Titus 3:10-11, we must turn away from the divisive ones. This kind of turning away is like the quarantining of a contagiously sick person. Because some of the saints were closely related to the divisive ones, their carrying out of this kind of quarantining is a suffering to them. Second John 10 says that we should not even greet those who are heretical in the teaching concerning Christ's divine person. Furthermore, 1 Corinthians 5:11 tells us that we should not even eat with a brother who is living in sin. Because of their close relationship with the divisive ones in the recovery, some of the saints have said that they cannot quarantine them. However, even though Miriam was Aaron's sister, he still had to quarantine her during the period of her leprosy (Num. 12:10-15). Hence, even to exercise to practice the proper quarantining is a suffering. We suffer because we do not like to see these dissenting ones separated from us. Nevertheless, if we do not quarantine them, we will not be doing the will of God, for we will annul the testimony of the oneness of the Body.

The Christian life is a suffering life because we must do the will of God. On the one hand, to do the will of God concerning our relationship with God is food to us. In John 4:34 the Lord Jesus said, "My food is to do the will of Him who sent Me and to finish His work." On the other hand, to do the will of God is a suffering.

The second reason for Christ's death is that He had to deny His human life in order to live by the Father's life. Like us, the Lord Jesus had a human life. When He was on the earth He did not live by His human life; rather, He denied His human life to live by the Father's divine life. First, we are people who do God's will. Second, like the Lord Jesus, we are people who do not live by our own life but by God's life. This too is a real suffering.

In every situation related to our daily living, we need to ask ourselves whether we are living by the divine life or by our natural life. If we do this, quite often we will realize that we are living by our natural life, our self. At such times we need to go to the cross (Luke 9:23). To go to the cross is to be conformed to the death of Christ. Even while eating our meals we need to be conformed to the death of Christ. At times we may be tempted to complain about the kind or quantity of food that we are given to eat. However, to complain is to live by the self, not by God's life. We are those who have been chosen, called, and sanctified by God to do His will. Doing the will of God is altogether a suffering to our natural life. Moreover, we are those who have been saved, regenerated, and separated to live not by our natural life but by the divine life. It is not a matter of whether we are doing something right or wrong; that is not the issue. The issue is, by what life are we doing it, by our natural life or by the divine life? To deny our natural life is a suffering to us. Every day and in every matter we struggle and fight with others to get what we desire. We like to do things by ourselves. To do something not by our life but by the life of another is a suffering. This is the Christian life.

CHAPTER SEVENTEEN

THE LIVING OF
THE PROCESSED TRIUNE GOD
AS THE CONSUMMATED SPIRIT

Scripture Reading: John 4:24a; Gen. 1:2b; Judg. 3:10; Luke 1:35; Matt. 1:18; Acts 16:6-7; Rom. 8:9; Phil. 1:19b; Exo. 30:23-25, 26-33; 1 John 2:20, 27; 2 Cor. 1:21; Luke 4:18; John 7:38-39; Rev. 22:1, 17a; 1 Cor. 6:17; Gal. 5:16, 25; Rom. 8:4b

I. THE CHRISTIAN LIFE BEING
THE LIVING OF THE PROCESSED TRIUNE GOD
AS THE CONSUMMATED SPIRIT IN THE BELIEVERS

In this message we want to see that the Christian life is the living of the processed Triune God as the consummated Spirit in the believers. If we know God only in an objective way, we will not know that God is the processed Triune God as the consummated Spirit. But if we have the subjective experience of God as the Spirit, we know that today God is the processed God.

We may have the assurance that God is our Father and that the Spirit indwells us. But how can the Triune God be our Father and how can the Spirit indwell us? Today we Christians have God as our Father and the indwelling Spirit because of the processes through which the Triune God passed in order to be dispensed into us.

The Triune God—the Father, the Son, and the Spirit— passed through the processes of incarnation and human living. In order for God to be our Father and for the Spirit to be the indwelling Spirit, the Triune God needed to be incarnated and live on this earth for thirty-three and a half years. Then He had to pass through death on the cross. If He had not died for our sins on the cross, how could God be our Father and how could the Spirit come to dwell in us? There would be no possibility of this.

The Lord went further to pass through the fourth process, the process of resurrection. On the morning of His resurrection, He told one of His lovers, "Go to My brothers and say to them, I ascend to My Father and your Father, and My God and your God" (John 20:17). After Christ's resurrection His Father became the Father of us, the believers. On the evening of the day of His resurrection, He breathed into the believers and said to them, "Receive the Holy Spirit" (John 20:22). He dispensed Himself as the Spirit into them after being processed through incarnation, human living, death, and resurrection. Through Christ's resurrection God is now our Father, and the Spirit is indwelling us.

Our Father is the processed Triune God, and the indwelling Spirit is the consummated Spirit. John 7:39 says that the Spirit was not yet because Jesus had not yet been glorified. Before Jesus' glorification in His resurrection (Luke 24:26), the Spirit was not yet, that is, He was not yet consummated, not yet completed. For the Spirit of the Triune God to come into us, there was the need of a consummation. He needed to be consummated to become the life-giving Spirit (1 Cor. 15:45b), that is, the pneumatic Christ. Then this pneumatic Christ, this life-giving Spirit, could become the indwelling Spirit within us.

The Christian life is to live the processed God as the consummated Spirit. This is according to our experience. What is the difference between us and the unbelievers? The difference is that we, the believers, have Someone within us. Who is this One within us? He is the processed Triune God as the consummated Spirit. The Triune God has been processed to be the consummated Spirit to live in us, the believers in Christ.

II. GOD BEING SPIRIT—
THE SUBSTANCE OF GOD'S BEING

John 4:24 says that God is Spirit. *Spirit* here refers to the substance of God's being.

III. THE SPIRIT OF GOD—GOD IN HIS MOVE

The Spirit of God in Genesis 1:2b refers to God in His move. Without being the Spirit, God cannot move. When God is moving, He is the Spirit. When a young man runs in a race, he becomes an athlete. The young man and the athlete are one person. When this young man does not exercise, he is just a young man. But in his running, in his move, he is an athlete. In like manner, God in His move is the Spirit.

IV. THE SPIRIT OF JEHOVAH— GOD IN HIS RELATIONSHIP WITH MAN

The Spirit of Jehovah is a particular expression, a particular divine title, ascribed to God in His relationship with man (Judg. 3:10). The title *Jehovah* is used frequently throughout the entire Old Testament, because the Bible is a book concerning God's relationship with His chosen people.

V. THE HOLY SPIRIT—GOD IN SANCTIFYING, SEPARATING MAN UNTO HIMSELF

The Holy Spirit is God in sanctifying, separating man unto Himself (Luke 1:35; Matt. 1:18). In the Old Testament, the title *the Holy Spirit* is not used. The title *the Spirit of His holiness* is used in Psalm 51:11 and Isaiah 63:10-11. *The Holy Spirit* as a divine title was used when Christ came to be incarnated. This indicates that Christ's coming in His incarnation is to get people sanctified, separated unto God. After Christ's incarnation, God sanctifies us, separates us, by coming into us and by bringing us into Him to mingle us together with Him. In this way man is fully sanctified unto God to be holy.

VI. THE SPIRIT OF JESUS—THE HOLY SPIRIT BECOMING THE SPIRIT OF THE INCARNATED JESUS

The Spirit of Jesus is the Holy Spirit, the Spirit who separates us unto God, becoming the Spirit of the incarnated Jesus (Acts 16:6-7). The Spirit of God, the Holy Spirit, has become the Spirit of Jesus. Today people talk much about following Jesus and imitating Jesus. But without the Spirit of Jesus, how could we imitate Jesus? Without the Spirit of

Jesus, we would be like lifeless robots in the Christian life. What makes us human beings is our human life and our human spirit. I have a human spirit, so I am a man. The animals do not have a spirit. The human spirit makes us particular. In the same way, because we have the Spirit of Jesus, this makes us Christians. This makes us particular people. The Spirit of Jesus is the Spirit of the Man Jesus with humanity that we may live the proper human life and endure its sufferings. By the Spirit of Jesus we share the Lord's humanity and its suffering strength.

VII. THE SPIRIT OF CHRIST—THE SPIRIT OF GOD BECOMING THE SPIRIT OF THE RESURRECTED CHRIST

The Spirit of Christ is the Spirit of God becoming the Spirit of the resurrected Christ (Rom. 8:9). By the Spirit of Christ, we partake of His resurrection life, His resurrection power, His transcendency, and His reigning authority.

VIII. THE SPIRIT OF JESUS CHRIST—THE SPIRIT OF THE PROCESSED AND CONSUMMATED TRIUNE GOD BECOMING THE ALL-INCLUSIVE SPIRIT OF THE INCARNATED JESUS AND THE RESURRECTED CHRIST

The Spirit of Jesus Christ is the Spirit of the processed and consummated Triune God becoming the all-inclusive Spirit of the incarnated Jesus and the resurrected Christ (Phil. 1:19b). To experience the Lord's humanity, we need the Spirit of Jesus. To experience the power of the Lord's resurrection, we need the Spirit of Christ. In his suffering the apostle Paul experienced both the Lord's suffering in His humanity and the Lord's resurrection. Hence, the Spirit to him was the Spirit of Jesus Christ, the compound, all-inclusive, life-giving Spirit of the Triune God.

IX. THE COMPOUND SPIRIT—THE SPIRIT OF GOD COMPOUNDED WITH CHRIST'S DIVINITY, HUMANITY, DEATH AND ITS SWEET EFFECTIVENESS, AND RESURRECTION AND ITS FRAGRANT POWER

The Spirit of God has been compounded. This is typified by the compound ointment in Exodus 30:23-25. This ointment is a compound of olive oil with myrrh, cinnamon, calamus, and cassia. The olive oil signifies the Spirit of God with divinity, myrrh signifies Christ's death, cinnamon signifies the sweet effectiveness of Christ's death, calamus signifies Christ's resurrection, and cassia signifies the fragrant power of Christ's resurrection. The one hin of olive oil also signifies the unique God, and the four spices of the plant life signify man, the creature of God. This, of course, refers to the humanity of Jesus, or to the Man Jesus. Thus, the compound Spirit is the Spirit of God compounded with Christ's divinity, humanity, death and its sweet effectiveness, and resurrection and its fragrant power. The one hin of olive oil compounded with four kinds of spices becomes a compound ointment for anointing.

Myrrh was used in ancient times to reduce the suffering of death. Cassia was a repellent used to repel snakes and insects. The power of Christ's resurrection is a real repellent. When you live in His power of resurrection, the devil and all the demons will flee away. We can have this experience when we are enjoying the infilling and the outpouring of the Spirit of Christ. When we are filled with the Spirit of Christ, we have the resurrection.

X. THE ANOINTING SPIRIT—THE COMPOUND SPIRIT WITH ALL HIS INGREDIENTS (ELEMENTS) BECOMING THE ANOINTING OINTMENT FOR THE ANOINTING OF ALL THE THINGS AND PERSONS THAT ARE OF GOD AND FOR GOD

It was with the compound ointment that the tabernacle and all its utensils and Aaron and all the priests were anointed (Exo. 30:26-33). Psalm 133 refers to this anointing ointment. Isaiah 61:1 says, "The Spirit of the Lord Jehovah is upon Me, / Because the Lord hath anointed Me...." In Luke 4:18 the Lord Jesus quoted this verse, showing that the anointing of Christ was by the Spirit. This can help us to realize that the anointing ointment signifies the anointing Spirit. Second Corinthians 1:21 says that God has anointed us, and 1 John 2:20 and 27 say that we all have received the divine anointing, the all-inclusive anointing, which teaches us in everything. The compound Spirit with all His ingredients (elements) becomes the anointing ointment for the anointing of all the things and persons that are of God and for God. The tabernacle with its furniture and the priests were of God and for God, so they were all anointed. Today the church with the saints has been anointed by this compound Spirit.

By all this we can see that the compound ointment in Exodus 30 is a type of the compound Spirit. God as the Spirit is typified by the one hin of olive oil, and this God has been compounded with Christ's divinity, humanity, with His death and its sweet effectiveness, and with His resurrection and its fragrant power. Today all these elements are in the compound Spirit. When we are filled with the Spirit, we have the deep feeling that we have been crucified. Furthermore, when we are filled with the Spirit, we have the deep feeling that we are resurrected. This tells us that within the filling Spirit are Christ's death and Christ's resurrection.

The Spirit today is an all-inclusive drink (1 Cor. 12:13; 10:4). This can be compared to a drink composed of water, tea, lemon, honey, and salt. This drink is a "compound" drink, a compound of five elements. When we drink this all-inclusive drink, we receive the elements of water, tea, lemon, honey, and salt. Likewise, when we drink the all-inclusive Spirit, we receive all of His elements into our being. This all-inclusive Spirit is God processed and consummated. He is the consummated Spirit as the consummation of the Triune God.

XI. THE SPIRIT—THE CONSUMMATED SPIRIT OF THE PROCESSED AND CONSUMMATED TRIUNE GOD AS THE CONSUMMATION OF THE TRIUNE GOD

Ultimately the Spirit of God is simply "the Spirit" (John 7:38-39; Rev. 22:1, 17a). The Spirit is the consummated Spirit of the processed and consummated Triune God as the consummation of the Triune God. Before the glorification of Jesus, the Spirit was not yet. But after Christ's resurrection, the Spirit of God became "the Spirit," the Spirit of the incarnated, crucified, and resurrected Jesus Christ. In Revelation 22:17a the Spirit and the bride speak together as one person. The Spirit here is the ultimate consummation of the Triune God.

In Romans 8:4 Paul said that we need to walk according to the spirit. The spirit here refers to the mingled spirit, which is the divine Spirit and our human spirit mingled together as one spirit (1 Cor. 6:17). Thus, the consummated Spirit of the processed and consummated Triune God indwells and has been mingled with our spirit.

XII. THE SPIRIT AND THE BRIDE

Revelation 22:17a speaks of the Spirit and the bride. This is the processed and consummated Triune God becoming one with the regenerated and transformed tripartite believers as the Body of Christ to be the universal couple for the expression of the Triune God in the redeemed and uplifted humanity (1 Cor. 6:17).

XIII. THE CHRISTIAN LIFE

The Christian life is that the believers in Christ have the processed and consummated Triune God as the substance of their spiritual being for their living in their daily walk (Gal. 5:16, 25; Rom. 8:4b). The processed and consummated Triune God as the consummated Spirit is our spiritual being. We live by the Triune God, walk by the Triune God, and do everything according to the Triune God.

Thus, we can see that the Christian life is the living of the processed Triune God as the consummated Spirit in us. This consummated Spirit includes Christ's divine and human person, Christ's death, and Christ's resurrection. All of the elements of Christ's person and work are compounded in this one consummated Spirit who is the consummation of the processed Triune God. He is triune; we are tripartite. He has been processed and consummated, and we have been regenerated and are being transformed. Eventually, He and we become a universal couple, and this universal couple will be the New Jerusalem for God's corporate expression for eternity. This is our Christian life.

ABOUT THE AUTHOR

Witness Lee was born in 1905 in northern China and raised in a Christian family. At age nineteen he was fully captured for Christ and immediately consecrated himself to preach the gospel for the rest of his life. Early in his service, he met Watchman Nee, a renowned preacher, teacher, and writer. Witness Lee labored together with Watchman Nee under his direction. In 1934 Watchman Nee entrusted Witness Lee with the responsibility for his publication operation, called the Shanghai Gospel Book Room.

Prior to the Communist takeover in 1949, Witness Lee was sent by Watchman Nee and his other co-workers to Taiwan to ensure that the things delivered to them by the Lord would not be lost. Watchman Nee instructed Witness Lee to continue the former's publishing operation abroad as the Taiwan Gospel Book Room, which has been publicly recognized as the publisher of Watchman Nee's works outside China. Witness Lee's work in Taiwan manifested the Lord's abundant blessing. From a mere three hundred fifty believers, newly fled from the mainland, the churches in Taiwan grew to twenty thousand believers in five years.

In 1962 Witness Lee felt led of the Lord to move to the United States, and he began to minister in Los Angeles in December of that year. During his thirty-five years of service throughout the United States, he ministered in weekly meetings, weekend conferences, and weeklong trainings, delivering several thousand spoken messages. His speaking has since been published, and many of his books have been translated into numerous languages. He gave his last public conference in February 1997 at the age of ninety-one and went to be with the Lord, whom he loved and served, on June 9, 1997. Witness Lee leaves behind a prolific presentation of the truth in the Bible. His major work, *Life-study of the Bible,* the fruit of his labor from 1974 to 1995, comprises over twenty-five thousand pages of commentary on every book of the Bible from the perspective of the believers' enjoyment and experience of God's divine life in Christ through the Holy Spirit. In addition, *The Collected Works of Witness Lee* contains over one hundred thirty volumes (over seventy-five thousand pages) of his other ministry from 1932 to 1997. Witness Lee was also the chief editor of a new translation of the New Testament into Chinese called the Recovery Version, and he directed the translation of the English New Testament Recovery Version. The Recovery Version also appears in over twenty-five other languages. In the Recovery Version he provided an extensive body of footnotes, outlines, and spiritual cross references. A radio broadcast of his messages can be heard on Christian radio stations in the United States and Europe. In 1965 Witness Lee founded Living Stream Ministry, a non-profit corporation, located in Anaheim, California, which publishes his and Watchman Nee's ministry.

Witness Lee's ministry emphasizes the experience of Christ as life and the practical oneness of the believers as the Body of Christ. Stressing the importance of attending to both of these matters, he led the churches under his care to grow in Christian life and function. He was unbending in his conviction that God's goal is not narrow sectarianism but the universal Body of Christ. In time, believers everywhere began to meet simply as the church in their localities in response to this conviction. Through his ministry hundreds of local churches have been raised up throughout the earth.

OTHER BOOKS PUBLISHED BY
Living Stream Ministry

Titles by Witness Lee:

Abraham—Called by God	978-0-7363-0359-0
The Experience of Life	978-0-87083-417-2
The Knowledge of Life	978-0-87083-419-6
The Tree of Life	978-0-87083-300-7
The Economy of God	978-0-87083-415-8
The Divine Economy	978-0-87083-268-0
God's New Testament Economy	978-0-87083-199-7
The World Situation and God's Move	978-0-87083-092-1
Christ vs. Religion	978-0-87083-010-5
The All-inclusive Christ	978-0-87083-020-4
Gospel Outlines	978-0-87083-039-6
Character	978-0-87083-322-9
The Secret of Experiencing Christ	978-0-87083-227-7
The Life and Way for the Practice of the Church Life	978-0-87083-785-2
The Basic Revelation in the Holy Scriptures	978-0-87083-105-8
The Crucial Revelation of Life in the Scriptures	978-0-87083-372-4
The Spirit with Our Spirit	978-0-87083-798-2
Christ as the Reality	978-0-87083-047-1
The Central Line of the Divine Revelation	978-0-87083-960-3
The Full Knowledge of the Word of God	978-0-87083-289-5
Watchman Nee—A Seer of the Divine Revelation ...	978-0-87083-625-1

Titles by Watchman Nee:

How to Study the Bible	978-0-7363-0407-8
God's Overcomers	978-0-7363-0433-7
The New Covenant	978-0-7363-0088-9
The Spiritual Man • 3 volumes	978-0-7363-0269-2
Authority and Submission	978-0-7363-0185-5
The Overcoming Life	978-1-57593-817-2
The Glorious Church	978-0-87083-745-6
The Prayer Ministry of the Church	978-0-87083-860-6
The Breaking of the Outer Man and the Release ...	978-1-57593-955-1
The Mystery of Christ	978-1-57593-954-4
The God of Abraham, Isaac, and Jacob	978-0-87083-932-0
The Song of Songs	978-0-87083-872-9
The Gospel of God • 2 volumes	978-1-57593-953-7
The Normal Christian Church Life	978-0-87083-027-3
The Character of the Lord's Worker	978-1-57593-322-1
The Normal Christian Faith	978-0-87083-748-7
Watchman Nee's Testimony	978-0-87083-051-8

Available at
Christian bookstores, or contact Living Stream Ministry
2431 W. La Palma Ave. • Anaheim, CA 92801
1-800-549-5164 • www.livingstream.com